My Mother, Me and My Wife

A cognizography in rambling realism

My Mother, Me and My Wife

A cognizography in rambling realism

V. Prakasam

ALLIED PUBLISHERS PVT. LTD.

New Delhi • Mumbai • Kolkata • Chennai • Bangalore • Hyderabad

ALLIED PUBLISHERS PRIVATE LIMITED

Regd. Off.: 1/13-14 Asaf Ali Road, **New Delhi**–110002
Ph.: 011-23239001 • E-mail: delhi.books@alliedpublishers.com

17 Chittaranjan Avenue, **Kolkata**–700072
Ph.: 033-22129618 • E-mail: cal.books@alliedpublishers.com

15 J.N. Heredia Marg, Ballard Estate, **Mumbai**–400001
Ph.: 022-42126969 • E-mail: mumbai.books@alliedpublishers.com

No. 25/10 Commander-in-Chief Road, Ethiraj Lane (Next to Post Office)
Egmore, **Chennai**–600008
Ph.: 044-28223938 • E-mail: chennai.books@alliedpublishers.com

P.B No. 9932, No.15, 3rd Floor (Next to Vijaya Bank), 5th Cross, Gandhi Nagar,
Bangalore–560009 • Phone 080-41530285/22386239
E-mail: bngl.journals@alliedpublishers.com/ apsabng@airtelmail.in

Sri Jayalakshmi Nilayam, No. 3-4-510, 3rd Floor (Above More Super Market)
Barkatpura, **Hyderabad**–500027
Ph.: 040-27551811, 040-27551812 • E-mail: hyd.books@alliedpublishers.com

Website: www.alliedpublishers.com

Revised Reprint, 2020

ISBN: 978-81-942903-0-8

Published by Sunil Sachdev and printed by Ravi Sachdev at Allied Publishers Pvt. Ltd., 1/13-14 Asaf Ali Road, New Delhi–110002

To
The ancient Rishi
Maharshi Kaundinya

Preview

Professor David G Butt
Linguistics Faculty of Human Sciences
Macquarie University, Sydney

Beware! This is a deeply profound book in a beguilingly simple form...Do not skip a page. Do not draw off thinking you have received "the message".

Yes, the main tenets of the work are declared outright: namely, the twin values of "TIME and RELATIONS" – what you give of your time and the significance of "only... connect" (to echo EM Forster). But the writing is not of a tract or self help guide. It is of family, of support in a world of human varieties—varieties of people, of cultures, of institutions, and of gods. And it is of love in a marriage; love which offers steady direction in a complex world.

At first, you may surmise the structure of the biography is whimsical. Well, you were told: "rambling realism". The generosity of a mentor might suddenly lead to an interregnum on grammars. The conscientious bus driver is an exemplum alongside the luminaries of learning—for example the spiritual guidance of Dr Ambedkar, or the intellectual vision of Professor SK Verma. A Telugu idiom may jump to a survey of English structures and how metaphors do or do not make sense to speakers of different languages. Translation is reviewed as involving different strategies. Professor Prakasam lived his life through the confluence of languages in India, and beyond in the UK and in America. He has had exchanges with leaders of international spheres of study: e.g. JR Firth and MAK Halliday from the UK; and Braj and Yamuna Kachru, MB Emeneau, and Noam Chomsky from America.

But, in the foreground is the family and his 53 years of marriage. "My Mother, Me and My Wife…" is a mesmerising read—it circles 'Time and Relations' as values from different perspectives, and first from the vignettes of the dignity enacted by, and expected from, all family members. The account challenges the zeitgeist so familiar in the utterances of populist politicians: for example, in my own country the expectation is ...well...you have to look after yourself, and you need to create a nuclear, domestic fortress against the world. The brief accounts of incidents at law (one of Prakasam's fields of doctoral study and specialist thought) are very 'telling'—i.e. thefts perpetrated against the household by outsiders are managed with a view to how the persons can be brought back to correct behaviour and how their futures can be developed, not blighted by punishment through the courts.

The wisdom of the women does seem akin to miraculous: what are the roots of its insights and eloquence. For it is not just the unconditional support and patience demonstrated by different generations of women, but their ability to capture the very essence of a situation in their words and expression. The time, for instance, when Prakasam uttered a mild criticism of his father-in-law, his mother takes him to task. Even the way she goes about it in three masterly verbal moves; so rhetorically effective that it is a moral exemplum that you can pass on, as well a moment from which one can learn. So too in his mother's characterization of the role of a husband to his wife, namely: that the husband had to replace all the love afforded by the parents and family that she has left in coming to the husband.

Intertwined in the family relations is the spirit of leaders of institutions, those advisers who sustained Prakasam in his formative years as a child, and later as a developing scholar and teacher. The 'method', if one desires such a designation, is of a spiral, a spiral of a self, of one who has been committed out to the immediate experiences of living: the lived particulars, the 'rambling realism' as it *"integrates different strands of reality"*. These strands and observations are unified by the effect they produce in the reader. A term from stylistics comes to mind. We become *naturalized* into a human landscape in which the ideologies and differences between people are treated as an abundance, not as a reason for anguish or conflict. For instance, there is no one God for Prakasam: all the Gods worshipped are forms of access to a unifying spirit to which one prays for common human reasons—the health of one's wife; courage in the face of misunderstandings. As an illustration of Prakasam's talent for presenting paradox and wisdom in a memorable style, I would ask the reader to reflect on the following:

> "*I always said that* the *Bhagavadgita is a social treatise on spiritual socialism and detached attachment.*"

Vignettes of family and professional life prepare us for this capacity to find what is sustaining, personal and egalitarian in the sacred without adopting divisions or exclusions based on ideologies or sub-communities. His own wordings follow a precept he applies to the tenets of valued texts, advice he calls "small unit autonomy":

> "*This is well utilized in scriptural texts to achieve what I call SMALL UNIT AUTONOMY (SUA). Believers tend to quote from scriptures and they will find it handy to do so if one-line or two-line units are self-sufficient*".

Let us consider the deep principles which the book introduces, and treat them as a more contemplative level of the lively "biography". First of all, the volume is called a "cognizography", not a biography—recall, also that the work is entitled: "My Mother, Me and My Wife:…" So Prakasam is the objective Me between the influences of two generations of gifted females. The author's reports are ways of realizing what endures about the legacy of two women and of the relatives who sustained his personality, his education, and his parenting. Like so many of the prominent poets of India and of the English speaking world, Prakasam seeks unity of mind and unity between personality and culture. For me, WB Yeats and TS Eliot are examples who come to mind. But they sought this kind of unity in turning to the past—myths of Ireland; Byzantium; the visions of Dante. By contrast here, Prakasam's unity is sought in the heartfelt particulars of direct experience of others: of his two female guiding spirits; of his strong uncles; of senior colleagues who take up his best interests in growing intellectually; of landlords who do so much for his life in London and York; of hosts in America. And more. The 'heartfelt' extends to the labyrinths of linguistic forms—these too are signs of universality found in the positive differences of your language for "being" (not just for "doing"). This response to the heartfelt particulars of actual lives is, in my view, so much more sustaining than any baleful appeals to the potentially factitious claims about an idealised past. Prakasam's life has confirmed his creed: look with goodness for goodness, and it may be found. Furthermore, in your language of "being" (the 'mother tongue' as we used to call it), your values and thoughts themselves demand reconciliation:

> "No thinking man's life is independent of what he is intellectually. His social, physical and mental constituents constitute his integrated self. The integrated self of an individual gives us his cognizography when he starts explaining for others. And this text is engendered by my integrated self.

Such then is the relational tenet around which this investigation of feelings is elaborated. It is the spiralling self that finds 'itself' through attention to others:

> "This spiralling self extends this concept to include others into it, whereas the cacoonian self treats others as unrelated."

A personal note here may accentuate the depth I sense in this and related statements. For c. 20 years, I have worked with psychiatrists who have focused on the language of therapy in the field of extreme disorders of personality. Much influenced by the thought of William James (1842-1910), they too have arrived at the metaphor of the "spiraling self", and the idea that one finds a health in the self 'between' people. Their work also describes the core of human development as stages of secure feeling. The central human systems— like the polyvagal system—are about an integration of felt experience.

The meaning of "cognizography" emerges. I venture that it is a form of secure, traditional wisdom reworked in a contemporary social topography, namely, in the contexts of modern people. It sometimes blends a modern idiom into a clause complex with SUA ("small unit autonomy"). Such blends are redolent with echoes of different sacred texts, from the Gita to a Christian bible: *"I always say let's follow 'no credit no debit policy' which means we are not responsible for our success or for our failure. Only we are responsible for our efforts and consequences."*

These concepts—spiraling self, cognizography—derive from a number of deeper principles which are both metaphysical and linguistic. The first might be "non-definability". The concepts and unities we pursue will always be 'ineffable'—just out of reach of our expressions in the same way that the categories of our meaning systems can never be totally commensurable with other explanations (e.g. from psychology or logic) or with the categories of another grammar. The best we can work with is another version, and another version, and so on. Consequently, all versions are to be given respect: "**non-definability** *is a part of our cognizance"*.

A similar deep gong is sounded when we read: "*Let us close this lengthy discussion of varna in the mentioned sloka with the generalization* **that identification subsumes differentiation**". This generalization is central to language, as it is in the interaction of cultures. A verbal equation brings two different elements in the very yoking that is unique identification: "(1) **She** is (2) **the love of my life**". A simple statement of an attribute—"She is intelligent"—differentiates and categorises. The linguistics of identification subsumes differentiation by showing that things unlike can be enjoined in a complex identity.

Let me conclude on Dr Prakasam's career as a teacher—his views on teaching and learning are a conduit of his giving to others. His insights need to be heeded by all who wish to contribute to the authentic development of learning. In this era of the corporate styled university, I hope that institutions can find their way back to his personal and practical wisdom:

> *The evaluation system should be a natural consequence of teaching strategies. It should never test 'memory'. It should allow the students to use books, collect facts from them and then organize their discourse. It is the discourse construction that is crucial in learning a language, not facts and figures.*

Inview

Professor ME Veda Sharan
Department of ESL Studies
The English and Foreign Languages University

My Mother, Me and My Wife: A Cognizography in Rambling Realism by Prof V Prakasam is a novel experiment, especially in the Indian context. Richly woven and taking palimpsests of impressions, the book is deeply philosophical, amusing, intimate, humorous, and a lot more. Prakasam's mind ranges over his life gathering up memories of successes, narrow escapes, academic excellence and travails, among a myriad other experiences. His story is the story of academicians, sons, teachers, researchers, fathers, husbands, and a lot more. His "rambling" is a freewheeling through life as it is lived. As his mind draws up reminiscences, he processes them into a narrative that is seemingly disjointed. But like the pieces of glass in a kaleidoscope, they turn and form ever new combinations of colour and design. They invite and challenge the reader to enjoy them *in vitro* and *in situ*—by each individual narrative and all together. Indeed, the three main characters in the title interact, exchange, and evoke ideas and emotions. They have, each one of them, sharply delineated personalities, and yet they blend and enrich other seamlessly.

Cognizography, as a genre, affords Prakasam a flexible, polyphonic platform where the narrative takes on features of an autobiography, a novel, a short story, anecdote, and philosophical meditations, among others. We see the primal struggle of tradition and modernity in his mother whose emancipation she owes to her own humanity and compassion as she ensures that a petty thief is forgiven on the grounds of his future potential. There are instances of life at crucial turning points where decisions have to be made with what TS Eliot calls "the awful daring of a moment's surrender". Surging patriotism enables the narrator challenge harsh and unwarranted words against his Motherland, even at the cost of a scholarship. Family bonds rise above short-term scholarships and have a happy ending. Life in all its variety, challenges, opportunities, frustrations, joys and triumphs converge in the book to make it as entertaining as it is enriching. The vignettes of life that Prakasam presents to the reader are drawn with honesty, accuracy, and truthfulness. The language of the novel, as befits a Professor of English, becomes a sort of Æolian harp that catches the smallest breeze and makes the most melodious music thanks to the authenticity of the narrative.

The vintage photographs that are included in the book lend it a pleasant charm and bring alive the persons in the cognizography. The writer's wife and mother come alive with their distinctive personalities. The story of the romantic affections between the narrator and his wife before and after marriage is a delicious blend of humour, tenderness, love, compromise and assertion and almost every nuance of emotion and feeling that humans are capable of.

There are large stretches of subjects dear to the writer's heart—linguistics, grammar, and the like. They may seem to be wandering away from the destination, but each is a "road not taken" that makes all the difference to the narrative. After all, a study of language is bound to be a study of life itself, for life is lived through language, and is constantly shaped by it to a degree we cannot fathom, or even realise.

The book will delight by its refreshing honesty, entertain by its vibrant narrative style, and continue to pull the reader towards it by its enduring mysteries hiding in the plain sight of psychology, language, and a love of life.

Review

Ravinder Gargesh
Professor (Retired)
Department of Linguistics
University of Delhi, Delhi

My Mother, Me and My Wife: A cognizography in rambling realism by Prof V Prakasam is an excellent creatively realistic manifestation of the author's cognisance of the meaningfulness of life from his childhood phase till the present. The narrative concerning the author's progress in life is encased between the narrative expressive of the gratitude to the highly positive and influential personality of the mother in the beginning and the highly understanding, intelligent and loving influence of the wife's personality at the end. The meaty middle part of the narrative brings out the growth of the child Prakasam from an initial explorer of life to a student, researcher, teacher, who simultaneously develops into a humane person steeped in the values of Dr BR Ambedkar, the great social reformer. The different narratives through the process stream of consciousness merge and fuse into each other giving us a richly textured discourse that celebrates Indian cultural values steeped in the concepts of universal brotherhood, respect for everyone, and the sanctity of close family relations. As a teacher and researcher of English and Linguistics, the narrator presents a logical exposition of some fundamental and crucial aspects of language and linguistics in socio-semiotic contexts, particularly through the theoretical perspective of the great linguist the late Prof MAK Halliday.

The book is dedicated to Maharshi Kaundinya, the ancient Indian scholar who had predicted that Prince Siddhartha would become the enlightened Buddha, and who was also the first to comprehend Buddha's teachings and become the first *bhikku*. The narrative in the form of the author's cognizing is divided into three sections—Section 1, Section 2 and Section 3.

Section 1 highlights the narrator's sense of egalitarianism which he draws from the *Bhagwad Gita*, the *Manusmriti*, the *Bible*, the *Quran*, and from the exploitation of Burukami in Japan, of Blacks in South Africa and in pre-civil war America. He relates the universal principles of equality, morality, sincerity, fair play and peaceful assertion of one's rights unaided by violence, nepotism and corruption, etc. to the great *Jnanayogis* and rebels of India, namely, Sri Krishna, Gautama Buddha, Guru Gobind Singh, Swami Vivekananda and Dr BR Ambedkar. He also believes that 'exclusive religiosity' is a problem whereas 'inclusive religiosity' is a blessing.

He acknowledges with gratitude the early mentoring by his mother and other elders of the family who inculcated in him a sense of sharing as well as the importance of the 'time and relations' management.

Section 2 deals with the personal development of the narrator from his birth in 1943 to the present time. Through the narration we trace his development from a simple child who considered the whole world to be speaking Telugu to his becoming an accomplished teacher of English language. He acknowledges with gratitude the contributions of his relatives, friends and teachers in his success. He moved from Nagpur to Hyderabad and then to the University of York, and then back to Hyderabad. It was initially at Hyderabad (CIE) where he was trained in the Hallidayan *Systemic Grammar* and he also came under the influence of Chomsky's *Transformational Grammar* and the classical Indian Theories of Meaning. He expresses particular gratitude to Prof SK Verma, who not only trained him in the Hallidayan model of linguistics but also charted his course as a researcher and teacher of English. His study and research at the University of York in UK further widened his horizons.

This section provides an interesting discussion of the languages of India. He talks about the development of various syllable based Indian scripts, such as the Sarada script in Kashmir and Punjab, the Gaudi in Bengali and Oriya, the Grantha script for Sanskrit, and the Tamil and Vattelettu scripts in South India, from the Brahmi script that evolved through the Ashokan and Gupta periods. His observations about the important role of English language in India today are pertinent. He believes that English in India over a period of time has been nationalized, and if properly utilised as a link language it will not disturb the basic strength of the Indian languages. His perspective on the form and function of languages is socio-semiotic in orientation. For example, certain forms have been creatively developed such as *prepone* as the opposite of *postpone*, and *stepbrother* as one's step parent's son by another marriage, or *half-brother* as the son of one's mother or father by another marriage, all depending upon our own contexts. Also, for the narrator, languages manifest variations not only in terms of dialects and sociolects but also on the basis individual usages and discourse features such as field of discourse (registers), mode of discourse (written versus oral forms) and the tenor of discourse (formal, informal, polite forms etc.).

For the narrator, English, Hindi, and Regional Languages have the status of languages of wider communication in India. Any of these languages could be used for official purposes within a state in India, and English or any of the Indian languages wherever they are used in countries like Sri Lanka, Singapore (Tamil), Bangladesh (Bengali), Pakistan (Urdu), Nepali (Nepali), Fiji, Mauritius (Hindi), etc. Besides this, India should go in for the recognition of Hindi as an international language and for its use at the United Nations.

The author's concern about the status of various Indian languages suggests a more objective criteria, such as population, for the selection of languages for inclusion in the Eighth Schedule of the Indian Constitution. He feels that there is a need to add languages like Bhojpuri, Avadhi, Adi, Ao, Bhili, Bodo, Dogri, Gondi, Halabi, Ho, Khandeshi, Kharri, Khasi, Khond, Kisan, Korkee, Koya, Kui, Kurukh, Lushai (Mizo), Ladakhi, Matlo, Munda, Mundari, Nissi, Santali, Savara, Sema, Tangkhul, Tripuri, Tulu and even English to the present 22 listed languages. This recognition will help in developing the feeling of one great land manifesting rich variety.

He looks at language from a linguistic perspective which is contrary to many commonly held stereotypes. For example, it is often believed that English has five vowels—a, e, i, o, and u. He dispels this misbelief by distinguishing between speech and writing, that the five letters of the alphabet represent many vowels which are defined as per distinctly identified sounds of speech. The variations existing between spoken forms and letters of the alphabet also include the letters *r, e, c, g, ch, ph, q, wh, x,* and *y*. Of special interest is the letter *s* representing plural form in words like *cats, boys and roses,* and their three respective spoken forms *s, z,* and *iz.*

The narrator also talks about the combination of sounds which through intonation and stress patterns lead to the formation of words and sentences according to a grammatical order, which in turn go on to form a coherent discourse. In the cognizing about language he also provides useful insights about the grammar of English, particularly in the context of verbs (tense and aspect), articles, adjectives, adverbs, anaphoric and cataphoric constructions etc. His discussion of the structure of English language is both for the teacher of English as well as for the translator and the creators of discourse in films.

Section 3 focuses on the contribution of the wife, his life partner for a very happy fifty three years, who had stood by him at all times with understanding and care, though she had constant health problems. She had read the *Ramayana* (in

Telugu) together with her husband and went on to co-author with him an abridged version of Valmiki's *Ramayana.* Her graceful behaviour personified the Indian concept of *maryada* that had allowed the author to flourish with dignity.

The overall writing style in the book is both subtle and witty. The author creates many expressions such as *muncle, maunt, puncle,* and *paunt* since there is no equivalent in the English language for the maternal uncle, maternal aunt, paternal uncle and paternal aunt respectively. He refers to English as *our National Foreign Language.* Some other expressions like *I think profusion of ideas leads to confusion awaiting fusion*, and his full forms for the abbreviated *UPS* as *Unpaid Primary Servant of the house*, or for a bad husband as the *Uninterrupted Pain Supplier*, and still further, for a good husband as *Uninterrupted Pleasure Supplier* etc. make the reading a pleasurable experience.

The book is excellent reading. It should be read by all students and teachers of English, particularly at the high school and undergraduate levels. The common reader will also find the book useful and interesting for its unique though simple way in which religious, philosophical, social and linguistic intricacies are resolved in the context of the present realities.

1

All of us have our mothers. Only a few very unlucky ones don't spend their life with mothers. I am among the lucky ones. I spent more than fifty four years of my life with my mother, who was guiding me and encouraging me all the time. I was born in 1943 and she left her mortal coil in 1998.

At every stage she is remembered by all of us, her children, their spouses, and her grandchildren. The qualities we remember and admire in her are sincerity, courage, efficiency, stoicalness, egalitarianism, fair play, and two interesting complexes: audi alteram partem complex and phoenix complex.

Socialness is the feeling we have for others in our society. This can be strengthened if we **love** others, **forgive** their faults and mistakes, be **compassionate** to all fellow beings and do our chosen or given **duty** well. If these five pillars of divine bliss are internalized by us, we will be enjoying the spiritual bliss of liberation, moksha, right in this life and that is what is called **jeevanmukti. Audi alteram partem** is a legal maxim which says, 'Hear what the other party says'. Without knowing this maxim my mother always said: 'look at it from the other person's angle'. I call it a positive complex because she would not judge any one just on the basis of someone's statement. Whenever as a child I reported to my mother against someone she would always say, "What did you do/say?" Same thing I followed while dealing with my children which they hold against me even now. The complaint is that I did not support them a priori, i.e., 'accepting without examination or analysis'. I think I was correct. If I was not, my mother would have to share the burden of the blame.

Egalitarianism is the belief or principle that all human beings are equal and are eligible for all the human rights.

She never made any distinction among workers or friends of her children on the basis of caste or religion.

The **Phoenix Complex** is the complex of someone who is of 'unique excellence, unsurpassable efficiency and very strong willpower'.

My mother lost her parents before she was five. She was brought up by two different sets of grandparents. This never disturbed her willpower and never made her either meek or sulky. She was always assertive and when the occasion demanded a bit aggressive too. She was always quick to learn, quick to correct herself, quick to decide and never believed in hidden agenda, nor played to the gallery, which we can shorten and sharpen as **galleried**. We can say she was a practising socialist, secularist and feminist without gallerying. I would certainly say with pride that she did her best to inculcate these qualities in her children and grandchildren. I remember once our neighbours were cutting a chicken and I saw it from our bathroom which was not 360 degrees closed. I asked my mother whether they could kill a chicken the way they were doing. She said that they were allowed to kill a bird to eat because they were non-vegetarians. She added that they could not kill for fun and on the other hand we are vegetarians and we are not allowed to eat any flesh.

Killing animals and birds and consuming them as food was very much there in ancient South Asia but there were a few rules. Hunting was allowed only for warriors and hunters by profession. Hunting, however, had attracted certain restrictions. One was not supposed to kill an animal when it was sleeping, when it was mating, when it was drinking water and when it was feeding its cubs. In other words, one was supposed to give it a chance to escape or defend itself. Similarly there were restrictions on killing animals essential for agriculture and warfare. Some people were told to eat only that meat which was offered in a **yajna** (sacrifice). They were also told not to perform a sacrifice just to eat meat. Similarly, some people were clearly told that they should not drink *sura* (liquor) but only smell it. So the ancient Indians were aware of the effect of meat and liquor on the human body, and restricted their use.

As a child, I had problems of health especially bowel movements, and also jaundice. My bowel movement ailments were corrected by our native rural Ayurvedic physician. My jaundice problem was twice corrected by a man called Krishnayya who was from one of the Scheduled Castes. He commanded respect from the whole village for his ability to cure certain ailments with herbal necklaces (*malas*), supported by mantras. I remember my mother telling me once that though my parents gave birth to me, it was Krishnayya who ensured my existence and I was exhorted to be grateful to him forever. It is very important to note that this person was highly respected because he healed several ailments of children and adults.

Egalitarianism was treated as an essential value in India but unfortunately it was subject to what Dr BR Ambedkar called Social Reality. On one hand people knew what Bhagavad Gita said and what Sri Krishna said to Uddhava in the Eleventh Chapter of the Bhagavat Puran. In the Bhagavad Gita Sri Krishna says to Arjuna:

> A scholar will look at a brahmana, a cow, a dog and the one who consumes it, with perfect understanding of equality. (Chapter 5:18)

The same idea is given to Uddhava by Sri Krishna in the Bhagavat Puran. But the problem was that this was subject to the social reality of caste hierarchy and untouchability. An interesting story in the Mahabharata confirms that varna-dharma actually led to division of labourers as Dr Ambedkar said. Yudhishthir asked Bhishma whether a brahmana could do business if he could not make his ends meet with Vedic studies. Bhishma responded saying that he could, but he should not sell meat, liquor, precious stones, and oils. How come? This rule was important most probably because it would not tempt the children of the brahmana to not go back to Vedic studies as the items mentioned would fetch huge profits. It might be that the intention also was to see that the brahmana should keep himself away from consuming liquor and meat and end up in overindulgence of pleasures.

However, one should not think that there was no flexibility in the system. Flexibility was there, but there was no scope for playing dual roles, except for social needs and state needs. In this context, it will be appropriate to remember that the Burukami of Japan was subject to social discrimination and the Blacks in South Africa, though in majority, were subject to discrimination during Apartheid regime. Similarly, Blacks were bought and sold in America before the Civil War. No religious ideology came to their rescue. Babu Jagjivan Ram made an enlightening remark when he said that there was no disturbance in India when Untouchability was abolished, whereas in America there was a Civil War when slavery was abolished. One might say that the American context had serious economic consequences whereas in India the social reality got adjusted which showed the awareness of oneness of human beings at the higher level though the practice of discrimination continued at the ground level. In different parts of the world, it is the aggressive modes of operation of the depraved which led to the suffering of the deprived. The depraved, unfortunately, became complacent about their sinful behaviour because it was after all a matter of praxis and would not affect the ideational purity of their spiritual being, or so they might have thought.

One may be wondering whether here we are justifying slavery and Untouchability. Certainly not. We are only trying to explain how depravity is a human phenomenon formed from the tendency to group for strength and grope for grandeur which is 'assumed self-importance'. The practical reality of work division lent its support to these activities. Beginning with a flexible and a practical division such things ended up as exploitative stability.

Coming from a village with the benign guiding hand of my mother, my mind was ripe to absorb the extremely influential philosophy of Dr Ambedkar when I was a lecturer in English at the Dr BR Ambedkar College of Arts and Commerce, Deeksha Bhoomi, Nagpur (1964–66). ***Ambedkarism is a blend of all that is great in human thinking. The principles of equality, morality, sincerity, fair-play and peaceful assertion of one's rights unaided by violence, nepotism and corruption constitute the core of Ambedkarism. For him, knowledge is the core of human existence and equality in every area is the core of social organization.***

In the village we can say that though farmers, we were also trained to be the students of knowledge. So the practical farming went hand-in-hand with attempts to acquire knowledge. This creation of opportunities to educate ourselves is now a widespread phenomenon in the villages producing brilliant professionals. No doubt this has to some extent affected the value given to farming. The redeeming feature is farming goes on though the farms change hands of ownership. The use of language has its social angle. The way we address someone is generally guided by the relationship we have with the other person. Unacceptable though it may be, we use vocatives reflective of their inferiority while calling some people. Thanks to my immersion in the principles of equality as enunciated by Dr Ambedkar, the expression orey (oh-rii) (characterised by impoliteness) disappeared from my Telugu speech.

One may seriously say that there are so many different types of people in this world, and how can we treat them as equal. Yes, there are let us say 1,44,000 types of people in the world, if we go by the stars (27), the planets (9), the constellations (12) and their combinations at the time of a person's birth. Let's not forget that planets constitute objective reality. God constitutes subjective reality. Sri Krishna says at the age of seven before he lifts Mt. Govardhan, that a man's life is guided by his nature and actions. Indra cannot change their luck.

This statement in Vyasa's Bhagavat purana (10th Skanda) gives a very rebellions thinking pattern of the seven years old boy. The differences among people are only physical, mental and economic. But socially and in terms of their human dignity they are the same. Human beings have similar needs and similar capabilities. People should not steal working help from someone and pay him or her low wages which is **labour theft.** Similarly we should not use natural resources more than what we need to. If we did it, we will be committing **resources theft.** Different prophets and thinkers guide us to keep away from both labour theft and resources theft. The Holy Quran exhorts us not to grab an orphan's property and not to cheat in terms of measurements. The Manu Smriti gives a clear injunction not to ignore the needs of parents and family members just to please others (chapter 11, shloka 10). The Holy Quran asks us to be grateful to parents (282, Sura 31:14).

Karl Marx very profoundly says that ultimately the difference between mental work and physical work will disappear. This mental work may take the form of scriptural explanations, writing books, teaching students, treating patients and planning constructions. Similarly physical work may take the form of some minor work like washing dishes and cooking or major works like constructing buildings and making cars. We have to take both types of labour with appropriate value and see that the wages meet the needs of people without any class distinction. Only then we can say there has been no labour theft or resources theft.

There is one more enemy to socialness, generally called **hedonism**, which is the belief that pleasure is the most important achievement. The practice of hedonism refers to people who indulge in seeking pleasure for themselves, especially their bodies. Such people tend to harm others not only in terms of resources but also in terms of their self esteem. This kind of **esteem theft** does greater damage to people, because it hurts them psychologically.

Egalitarianism is thus a social need but not just a fashionable creed, nor a private virtue. Labour theft, resources theft, esteem theft and denial of opportunities to grow are abhorrently unacceptable. Treating all as equals, providing equal opportunities for them to grow and treating all sections of people with equal care, compassion and consideration is egalitarianism.

We may add a couple of words regarding the phoenix complex. A strong willpower which fights against false criticism, occasional failure, discouragement, taunts, non-availability of resources and all other negativities that look into your eyes is phoenix complex. A good individual is one who tries to instill this quality in any person that approaches him or her with fear and depression. A bad person is one who tries to make other person feel that it was inevitable and cannot be redeemed. This kind of attitude is harmful to both the advisor and the advisee.

Two very important aspects of socialness are: awareness of the needs of our fellow human beings and the desire to share our resources with them. And here again my mother was a great guide to me by teaching me the quality of sharing what I have with the others. The sharing may be in the form of giving academic help, goods and correct guidance. One should be very clear about the fact that unless you think about others, care for others and share with others you absolutely have no right to expect help from others when you need it. And an interesting fact to note in this context is that the academic sharing is twice blessed the way Shakespeare said that mercy was twice blessed (The Merchant of Venice). Mercy no doubt blesses the one who shows it and also the one who is shown, benefiting him or her. Similarly academic sharing blesses the beneficiary and also the benefactor by strengthening their knowledge. The most fascinating part is, sharing here does not lead to any physical transfer of knowledge but only creation of the same body of knowledge in the beneficiary. Actually this creation of knowledge in the beneficiary is facilitated by the benefactor without parting with anything, without having to make any sacrifices.

Egalitarianism also involves understanding of variant reflections of the basic phenomenon. Divinity is understood differently by different cultures leading to different religious groupings. Any religious doctrine which says that God is pleased only with a particular group and He will let only them into heaven is in a sense **communal religiosity** and **exclusive religiosity**. To think that God is not impartial and to think God likes only a particular group of people and to think God will punish all those who do not belong to a particular group is nothing but blasphemy and on the other hand considering different types of prayers practised by different groups will reach the same Almighty is **secular religiosity**. This is **inclusive religiosity**. This kind of thinking is propagated by Bhagavad Gita and Bhagavad Puran where Krishna tells Uddhava as much. I remember on a Sunday I asked my mother's permission to go to a church. This was when I was in Kavali and I was doing my MA at Nagpur. Occasional visits to church were the result of the influence of my best friend BJ Premasagar on me. One may wonder why anyone needs mother's permission at that age. Well, that was my family culture. We always took parent's permission when we went out. This I continued in the form of giving information to my wife whenever I went out. Now back to my mother's permission. My mother said I could go if I wanted to pray there and added that God receives our prayers in whatever form as long as we are sincere. This is secular religiosity. Well, this is common with our family because they use to visit a Dargah in AS Peta (also called Rehamatabad) in Nellore district. This is the tradition set by Bhagavad Gita in Chapters 4, 5 and 6.

Looking at workers with special care was one thing I didn't appreciate in the beginning. My mother used to give a special pack of rice for one worker where general food was lumps of ragi (sangati). I took it as an instance of partiality. When she explained the situation I realized it was care conditioned by the special situation. This particular boy had a stomach problem which was aggravated by ragi whereas rice suited him. This is individualizing care. Actually the Indian tradition says *dharma* always varied on the basis of deśa (area), kāla (time), samāja (society), all was this no doubt guided by *yuga dharma*, i.e., dharma of the given age. It was in this context, we can happily remember what BR Ambedkar, one of the greatest intellectors of the world said: 'there is no finality in thinking'. But it should be remembered that this non-finality is not caused by mercenary or political interest nor by physical harm. It is guided by **continuous ideational activity**.

This kind of differential care was part of my mother's personality. I remember her advising a Telugu lady in Patiala not to snub her son too much. She said when we snub a boy often he begins to believe that the negative things you say about him are correct and will not grow beyond them. On the other hand a normal girl will not easily be intimidated. Let's be clear about one thing here: all generalizations leak, and all generalizations are subject to the rider: ceterus paribus, i.e., other things being equal. It looks as though a good government guided by an intelligently worded constitution ensuring the rule of law is like a good mother dispensing strong, disciplining, individualizing care and ensuring growth of every individual. We have to look at the reservations in school admissions, job openings and elected posts from this angle. All people haven't had equality of opportunities in academic, economic and administrative fields. The have-nots actually were denied access to different resources for social causes. In one sense the haves have had reservations for them in the name of knowledge and merit. It is high time that the have-nots should be empowered in all areas. This certainly includes reservations for women of all social groups. Only then the ideated egalitarianism becomes egalitarianism in praxis.

My mother always believed in giving Caesar his due. She said that whatever we are enjoying now is due to the generous donating and sharing practices of my paternal grandfather Vennelakanti Venkata Ramanaiah. Sometimes he would forego his meal for someone and then wait for the food to be prepared for him later. This *dana* and *dharma* my mother said we should also practise to ensure that our grandchildren would be in right state of life.

Several uncles and aunts played their roles in our lives. These two words of English are not properly significative of our kinship relations. Maternal uncle (muncle) has one role to perform and paternal uncle (puncle) has a different role to perform. So I use words like muncle, maunt, puncle, and paunt. A puncle of mine was a kind of genius. He always thought differently from others. He was a school teacher but with a lot of re-thought-out traditional knowledge and my mother always preferred her children and grandchildren to be initiated into learning by him. Learning-initiation is called *aksharābhyāsa* and the one who does it is called *guru* and my guru was my puncle Ramakrishnaiah. I saw to it that he also became guru of my son Gautam. Each puncle has a contribution to make in the development of the personality of an individual, especially in a joint family. My youngest puncle Hanumanthrao instilled in me the principle of refraining from copying in an examination. The way he instilled it in me reflected his temper too. When he was told that I had copied in an exam he gave me a strong slap and said, "Fail if you have to, copying you should never." My last-but-one puncle Srinivasarao became my model in generosity and happy disposition. My mother always said it was this puncle who inherited the virtue of generosity from my grandfather.

Now comes my muncle. I had only one muncle, Akkaraju Subrahmanyam. A fairly rich, tactful karanam (village accountant). He had no children. He took a lot of interest in our family and helped us come up in life. After my pre-University course the time came for my joining an undergraduate course. My anna (senior brother) was to join an engineering course. The family could not support two college-going children. They wanted me to stay home. I protested. I did Satyagraha. I refused to eat, I was pretty rhetorical: "When you have two eyes do you give pinpricks to one eye?" Saying this I went on a hunger strike. My muncle who was away in my district town, Nellore, came back and told my mother that he would put me in the college. He had heard of, while in Nellore, a boy committing suicide because he was not sent to the college. When I look back, I can say that he monitored my undergraduate tenure very closely in all respects.

Right in the first year I chose a room for my stay which, I was unaware, was a home of call girls. My roommate who had invited me to stay with him was probably aware of it. My muncle who visited me smelt the reality and shifted me right away to another known person's room in another house. Obviously that saved me from going off the expected track. There is another interesting incident worth mentioning. I was doing my BA (Spl) with English literature and Telugu literature and Modern European History besides the general subjects of English, Telugu, and General Education. I was a student of VR College Nellore, in 1958–61. I think in the second year I played the role of Mark Antony in Julius Caesar which was staged as part of the college festival. This was well-planned and directed by one Pattabhirami Reddy. Pattabhirami Reddy, Premasagar, Prakasam we were called the 3Ps because we were always together even when we missed our classes. A cousin of mine—actually a paunt's son—saw the play and appreciated it. He mentioned it to my muncle when he met him, deeply appreciating my acting. The next morning my muncle was there in the college before I went there. He looked at me curtly and said, "You are in this college for studies, not for acting", and went off. That was it. No question of acting further. His command was like a commandment.

I also remember how he used to send me money. He asked one bus driver to handover 5 rupees to me. My muncle gave him money at Kaluvaya, in those days called Firka headquarters, being a revenue area, now called Mandal, a developmental Panchayat term. The driver stopped the bus with its passengers at a point which was close to where I was staying (Raghavareddy Building, Yedlavari Street, off Trunk Road). He came all the way to my room and gave me money. Someone who is living in 2019 cannot properly assess the value of 5 rupees. If you look back, with 5 rupees we could buy 40 plates of idly or 40 cups of coffee in those days from a grade B restaurant. If we see how much we need to buy 40 plates of idly or 40 coffees we know the value of 5 rupees today. Sometimes I wonder how our elders guide us. I remember when I was seventeen, hair started growing on my cheeks and chin. I just ignored them. Again it was my muncle who advised me to start shaving. I think we should remember with appreciation the care our elders show in our growth, the support they give us in our development and the guidance they give us to tread the right mill, I mean path.

Coming back to my village and my mother, I would like to say that several other women in the village used to like my mother, help her and receive help form her. I remember one lady, Ram Subbamma who used to call my mother akka (elder sister). One day I came back from somewhere and she saw me entering our house. Within ten minutes she came with a tumbler of fresh buffalo milk and told my mother to make me some coffee. When I mentioned it to my sister recently she said that the lady used to do something else for her. She would always bring a small cup of ghee and say to my mother 'serve her this ghee'. This shows the village love for friendly neighbours. About five years ago I had a dream in which Ram Subbamma warned me about my neighbours who were working in our house as servants. I was surprised how from such a distance and at such an advanced age of 95–96 she thought of us and warned us in the dream. Lo and behold! Her warning became a reality. The neighbour boy who used to come to clean the house coolly stole more than ten thousand rupees and a mobile instrument. That boy was a very bright boy in school and he was getting A and A+ in his tenth class. So I decided to not disturb his career by raising a hue and cry or approaching the police. I also felt I was equally to blame by making the money accessible to people who could be tempted. This is what Milton said in his Areopagitica. I just prayed to Sri Ram Sir, a professor of English known to have a touch of divinity. Within five minutes the boy's sister and mother came to my house and owned the theft and returned the instrument. They also offered to work for four months without any salary in lieu of stolen money. I didn't want any free work. But they insisted on atoning for the theft. They also mentioned that the boy stole the money for betting on cricket. It is very important to remember our sense of justice should be guided by people's welfare rather than by rigorous implementation of a rule. In Plato, this same idea about justice being shaped by the situation is described as being 'architectonic'.

This incident of ignoring your loss and protecting the culprit's welfare seems to be a repeat of another incident more than 20 years ago. A painter in my house stole my daughter's watch. On my complaint the police took him away. After a couple of hours my mother asked me to withdraw the case because the frail looking boy would collapse if the police beat him up. She added that we could buy a new watch. This kind of compassionate consideration I obviously inherited from my strong but kind mother.

Interestingly my mother had seen both 'plentifulness' and 'emptifullness' but it never disturbed her equanimity. She also seemed to have the idea that human beings are more important than their wealth and status. In my own sermonic style I always say only two things matter in life: TIME and RELATIONS. These two constitute human life. And real success lies in the management of time and relations. Money is only a source to keep things going, to take care of our needs and to ensure exchange of work with resources. The one who seeks money for money's sake is not fully equipped with human value system.

I always say money in the pocket or in the bank is beneficial whereas money in the brain leading to depression, anxiety or false ego is disastrous.

Both my mother and father were very kind to my wife who was a heart patient. I used to tease them saying that they were tactful to ensure regular supply of coffee and food. My mother would call me 'abbayya' (boy, the way son is called in Telugu) at 10 in the night. This is for her cup of Bru coffee. Now and then I teasingly said, "Ask your daughter-in-law" but mother would say that she should be allowed to rest. At 6 in the morning my father would call me 'Prakasam!' asking me to make him a cup of filter coffee. Sometimes here also I would teasingly say 'ask your daughter-in-law'. He would say 'no, no don't disturb her'. All this care and caution were in a sense warranted. Because she underwent a double valve replacement in 1992, which was preceded by Mitral valvatomy in 1981, and followed by hernia correction and hysterectomy in 1996.

My mother was a practising feminist, not a gallerying one though. One day I made a negative comment on my father-in-law while speaking to my wife. My mother asked me how I would react if my wife had said something negative about my father. I said I would become angry, and then she said: "Then who gave you the right to criticise her father?" She was in a sense a special person. My anna (elder brother) once said that she belonged to the next century not the present (20th) century. On another occasion she said: "A good husband is one who replaces for his wife the love her parents and siblings have for her, because she leaves them to join the husband." Can anyone give more sermonic definition of a husband?

I certainly would not hesitate to relate something which has negative flavour. My muncle used to make fun of considerate husbands saying, "Useless fellow, he massages his wife's calves!" This statement he used to give about others. When I was around 50 or so, already a grandfather, I summoned my courage and very coolly said: "Muncle, better for the husband to do it, than a man from the neighbourhood." He understood the importance of the message and responded: "Correct, this never occurred to me." One can see how my muncle and mother differ in this respect. Otherwise they were equally generous, efficient and disciplinarian, characterized by 'dakshata'.

Both my mother and muncle were given to recommending appropriate speech quantitatively, qualitatively and ontologically. My mother always quoted a Telugu saying, 'nōrā, veepu daggara' (hey mouth, the back is closeby). In other words, it says, 'wrong speech invites punishment'. When I think of it I remember what is given in the Bible (Mathew 15:11, 17–20):

> Not that which goes into the mouth defileth a man; But that which cometh out of the mouth, that defileth a man (11)... whatever enters in the mouth goes into the belly and is cast out into the drought, but those things which proceed out of the mouth come forth from the heart; and they defile the man. For out of heart proceed evil thoughts, murders, adulteries, fornications, thefts, false witness and blasphemies. These are the things that defile a man but to eat with unwashen hands defileth not a man [17–20].

The Bible is great because it has great statements in it and Lord Jesus is great because he said such things. Had he preached things which are harmful to the people we would not have treated him as the Saviour and the Son of God. In this context, I am reminded of what my botany teacher, Padma Abraham wrote in the autograph she gave me in 1958:

> 'Word is not a bird
> Once you let it fly
> You cannot whistle it back again'.

A friend said that this was also from the Bible.

Similarly see what the Bhagavad Gita says:

> Self-realized sages perceive alike—
> A learned and humble Brahmin, a cow,
> An elephant, a dog and a dog-consumer (Chap V:18).

We don't want to know the class of birth of Ved Vyasa's mother or father nor of Sri Krishna to evaluate the greatness of this statement.

All this is possible if one thinks, and thinks sincerely. The real term is 'intellecting'. An intellectual is one who 'intellects'. Intellecting is meditating on a subject, with a view to arriving at its epistemology, i.e., its origin, nature, and applicability. The one who intellects a subject and expresses his findings 'without fear or prejudice' becomes a Jnanayogi. The one who does it regarding different subjects like Anthropology, Sociology, Politics, Law, History, Economics, Language, Religious Texts and Religious Doctrine is a real MahaJnanayogi. This Maha Jnanayogi is Dr BR Ambedkar. The other great Jnanayogis of India are Sri Krishna, Gautam Buddha and Swami Vivekananda. Similarly the great rebels of India are Sri Krishna, Gautam Buddha, Guru Govind Singh and Dr BR Ambedkar. These great Indian minds show both ideationally and in praxis new modes of thinking and living. One may ask how would one call Sri Krishna a rebel. Just let's get back to the great anecdote of raising Mount Govardhan and holding it up for a week. Before doing it he said to his foster father Nanda: "A man's life is guided by his Nijasvabhava (his self-disposition) and his karma (action). Indra cannot change his adrishta (luck)." A seven year old boy saying this about an established divine entity is a great act of cognitional rebellion. If one intellects properly one can realise that Krishna was taking us away from **Yajnamarga** (of a few) and putting us on **Jnanamarga** (of all).

It can also be said that at the age of seven the human child becomes conscious of himself and his environment and starts enquiring into what is happening. It is clearly said that the teacher should allow his students to ask questions once they reach the age of sixteen. Same advice is given to a father to allow his children to ask questions. Islam also rightly says that the age of sixteen is the age of adulthood. Seven to sixteen seems to be the age of enquiring, seeking information, consolidating whatever is collected. Sixteen is obviously the time a person can participate in a discussion. Now I remember an incident. My son was having his breakfast when I think I said something which was kind of kid stuff. He responded tersely. My wife looked at me and said: "He is sixteen now." I could immediately realise that he had freedom to disagree with me.

One should not forget that speech, a very complex communication system humans are gifted with, should be aptly made use of. Economy of communication should not be entropic, which is non-availability of signals for communication. Nor should it be characterised by redundancy—the over-abundance of communication signals. Redundancy will be in order with a story telling text for children and also texts instilling moral values. Some of these statements are quoted out of context sometimes in single line. To achieve Small Unit Autonomy redundancies are unavoidable. Similarly repetition becomes important for drilling—for making a point sink into the youthful mind. On the other hand entropy will not be out of place in riddles, proverbs and religious commandments.

The discussion of entropy and redundancy brings an important point for us to focus on. Every word has its intrinsic meaning-bearing potential caused by several decades of use. These words acquire new dimensions though, whenever life styles change. A professional user of language cannot afford to use it unduly casually. We have already used words like *communal*, *secular* and *religiosity*. If they are not properly decoded, the users of language may not get the right import of a given message. Let's now look at the definite values of words like *secular*, *communal*, *religious* and *devout*.

Let us start with the word 'community' which is 'a group of people living together and/or united by shared interests, religion, nationality, language, etc.' 'Communal' as a derived adjective is not very 'harmful' per se. It is defined as follows: 'of, related to, or based on social, religious, or language groups'. Longman's English Larousse has interestingly added a second definition: (India) of religious or social communities (e.g. 'communal riots').

These definitions do not really help us explain the use of 'communal' in expressions like 'he is communal'. Somehow in our country 'communal' is used in connection with religious prejudices and the consequent behaviour. To do justice to the term we have to include religion, caste (including sub-caste) and language as the communal parameters in the context of the complex pattern that emerges in India. The menaces of caste communalism and creed communalism are more pronounced than language communalism. This trinity of communal attitudes has been a plague on our society. The tragedy is that religion, caste, and language are not responsible for the prejudices. It is the narrow-minded individuals and groups that exploit a particular parameter for their personal benefit. In our context 'communal' can be defined as follows:

> "Conscious of the distinction of individuals on community lines with a view to safeguarding the interests of a community and acting in a prejudiced way against the members of other communities."

One can see that the institution of community which is the product of the historical evolution of the society is the 'basis' for communalism, not the 'cause' of it. The socio-political behaviour of the individual is the result of 'nurture' more, and less of 'nature'. In other words, no individual is 'communal' because he is born in a particular family, i.e., communalism is not 'hereditary'. 'Communalism' is the result of 'ignorance' or an 'intellectual vacuum'. Generally the people who hurt members of other communities are the ones who are ignorant, ill-bred and ill-motivated. The shoulder on which the gun of communalism is placed is the 'community', but it is not the gun itself. The gun is selfish and prejudiced thinking, which is the offspring of ignorance. For example, anyone who understands the principles of a religion will never spill blood in its name. 'Communalism' is the antithesis to religion.

Now a word about caste here. Irrespective of one's religious affiliation, an average Indian somchow belongs to a caste. He is as fervent about it as the white man is about his race. There is a wrong impression both here and aboard that Hinduism, the religion as such, is responsible for the caste system and the abhorrent phenomenon of 'Untouchability'. This is due to confusion between the socio-political system of the country and the professed or accepted religious philosophy. No one can hold Christianity responsible for the racist philosophy of apartheid in South Africa. Similarly no one can hold Buddhism and Shintoism responsible for the problems of the Burakumin, the outcastes of Japan. An interesting parallel could be established between the four-tier caste system of ancient India and Japan. The Brahmans, Kshatriyas, Vaishyas and Shudras constituted the four tier caste system. The fifth caste—the panchamas referred to people treated as untouchables. With the passage of time new castes and subcastes emerged in different parts of India. Interestingly the caste-system also got revised and what we see in modern India is not at all similar to what is described in the Puranas and other books of the ancient days.

Look at the system operating in pre-modern Japan:

> The elementary histories describe well the pre-modern four-tier class system of Japan with the Samurai, the warrior administrators acting as the political elite and governing a large peasant population of agriculturalists forming the productive backbone of the country. Ranked beneath the farmers were the artisans, or specialists with

various technical skills, and (officially at least) in fourth status level, the merchants.

These four 'human' classes had beneath them groups of lowly 'sub-human'. These included the 'Hinin' literally 'non-people', a heterogeneous group comprising of beggars, prostitutes, fugitives from justice, itinerant entertainers, mediums, diviners and religious wanderers who had fallen right out of the class system. Beneath even this group were the 'genetically impure' Eta whose occupations were ritually polluting. Some worked with leather and killed animals, eating their meat. They handled the dead and acted as executioners of criminals. Others worked in hereditary crafts such as basketry which, for forgotten reasons, had become classified as the monopoly of the hereditary outcastes.

'The origins of these occupational groups are shrouded in history. The most acceptable theory is that the concepts of pollution already existing in indigenous Shinto beliefs were reinforced and modified by Buddhist concepts related to the impurities attributed to killing and eating meat' (Japan's outcastes—the problem of the Burakumin, by George A Devos, (1971) London: Minority Rights Group Report No. 3, pp. 4–5).

We cannot hold Shintoism and Buddhism responsible for the problems of Japan's 'out-castes'. Similarly we cannot hold Calvinism responsible for the mistakes of the State of South Africa where a liberal society got divided and balkanized in the second half of 20th century. Whereas in India there has been a consistent effort to get rid of the social evils, the Immorality Act of South Africa passed in 1949 prohibits marriages across different races: Whites, Coloureds, Asians and Blacks. Again an interesting parallel—here the Chinese, the Japanese and other 'Yellow' people were given honorary white status in South Africa. In ancient India several foreign invaders got Kshatriya-status when they came to settle in India.

It is a sad fact of history that socio-political institutions pollute religious institutions and bring them a bad name. If caste differences exist among people of different religions in India, one can easily see it as a social problem, not a problem of religious heritage.

In India 'caste-communalism' is more widespread and deep-seated than 'creed-communalism'. Academic institutions, professional bodies, political parties including the so-called progressive parties are contaminated by caste communalism. I know of many atheists and irreligious people who are downright communalists with regard to 'caste'.

The cause of communalism of whatsoever type is the void in the knowledge sack of man. One who is well-entrenched in any of the religious philosophies or humanist philosophies can never be 'prejudiced'. I go a step further: 'ignorance engendereth all evils' including fear and prejudice.

Religion is 'a system of beliefs and practices relating to the adherents in a community'. A religious person is one who is 'faithful in religion, who obeys the rules of religion very carefully'. A person who is 'well behaved according to the rules of religion' is said to be God-fearing.

A devout person is one 'who attends to religious duties sincerely and earnestly'. It goes without saying that a religious-minded person, a God-fearing person or devout person is more concerned with his own thinking and behaviour and cannot afford to be communal.

An orthodox person is one 'who conforms to or holds the official, accepted or standard behaviour and opinions'. An orthodox person is not necessarily a devout person. A devout person is not so much concerned with the official acceptance. Similarly a devout person may or may not be orthodox.

A heretic is one 'who holds a belief against what is accepted especially in official religion'. One should never think that a heretic is necessarily non-communal or liberal. A nonconformist is one 'who does not conform to the beliefs or rituals of an established creed'. Here again his deviation is in attitudes and behaviour. This does not guarantee against his being carried away by the considerations of the interests of his community. An atheist is one 'who denies the existence of God, particularly with regard to theistic formulation'. If the lack of moral considerations of religious philosophy is not compensated for by humanistic values, an atheist again might get subjected to parochial interests of group affiliation problems. The same holds good in the case of an agnostic (a person who thinks that nothing can be known about the existence or nature of God) or a sceptic (a person who is sceptical about the claims of a religion).

A fanatic is one 'who is an inordinately zealous adherent or supporter in religion (or politics)'. He is a person 'who shows very great and often unreasoning keenness for some religious (or political) belief'. A fanatic may or may not be orthodox but he can never be 'devout' in the real sense of the term. A devotee is a simple soul but a fanatic is a politicised person. A devout person can never be fanatic. A fanatic may ultimately 'fall' to become a bigot: 'a person who thinks strongly and unreasonably that his own belief or opinion is correct; he is obstinately and intolerantly devoted to his own beliefs, creed or party'. A bigoted person is 'narrow-minded and prejudiced'. A bigot tends to be communal, but all the communal fellows need not be bigoted. The bigoted fellow believes in something strongly but a communal fellow need not believe in anything at all except his own or his group's interests. Similarly, a communal fellow may not be fanatic, he may not be really supporting any ideology. One should also make a distinction between 'genuine communalists' and 'pseudo-communalists'. A genuine communalist is one who is psychologically weak and intellectually blank and really prejudiced and narrow-minded. A pseudo-communalist is one who is not at all prejudiced but uses communalism to his pecuniary and personal advantage or for political or social power. It may sound paradoxical at first sight but it is a fact that the pseudo-communalist is more dangerous to the peace of society than the genuine communalist. This is like 'you can never wake up someone who is not really asleep'. You can disabuse a genuine communalist of his narrow-minded views by widening his cognitive horizon with the help of religious or humanistic philosophy. But you can never educate the pseudo-communalist because he is not a communalist. He is just using it as a tool for a different purpose. He will never listen to your argument and no philosophy will enter his steel helmet of selfishness. There is only one type of hope in his case—a nerve-racking experience which shocks him out of his shell of selfishness and greed.

Let's now see what is meant by being 'secular', the antonym of 'communal' in the present context. In English the word 'secular' means, 'not connected with or controlled by religion, not religious; of matters related to the world rather than with religion'. But in our socio-political context it has to be defined vis-à-vis 'communal'. A secular person is one 'who does not bring into his socio-political dealings the considerations of his group-membership'. A secular doctor, for example, treats all his patients alike without the consideration of group affiliations. A secular teacher treats all his students alike. A secular politician is one who does not believe in or exploit group identity in his political dealings. A thoroughly religious-minded, God-fearing and devout person is bound to be secular in the sense given here. But a secular person may not be a religious-minded person. Secularism as a positive mental attitude must be used by all of us who want to be members of a given society. That does not mean we don't follow our religious practices though we should give up practices which harm fellow human beings and environment.

As we had mentioned earlier gallerying secularism is not always genuine secularism. It tends to be sectarian secularism guided by political correctness and vote bank politics. A sectarian secularist harps on the wrong practices of one community, whereas in the name of not hurting the feelings of the members of another community he never criticises the wrong practices of that community. One should also be very clear about one thing: secularism treats all people as equal without any distinction made on the basis of creed (religious sect) or caste. Interestingly, some dangerously casteist leaders gallery about secularism. Both caste and creed are part of social reality and there is no need to ignore them. But it is absolutely essential for human happiness to not drag them into public life for creating differences among people.

We can ensure human happiness if we fill our thinking with love for fellow human beings. That will save us from false ego and exclusivist behaviour. One of the important qualities of my mother is 'not being fussy'. Here I bring in two sentences Noam Chomsky, one of the great linguists world has seen, made very famous:

> John is easy to please.
> John is eager to please.

These two constructions interestingly can be applied to my mother in different ways:

> My mother is easy to serve and please because she is not fussy.
>
> My mother is eager to help and serve because she is good at heart.

This 'is easy' refers back to my mother as the recipient of 'serve and please'. In 'is eager' the recipient of 'help and serve' will be 'the others', not mentioned. But in both the sentences it is the nature of my mother that is being talked about: 'Not being fussy' and 'being good at heart'. It is this nature sometimes can effect or affect others' behaviour. I used to tease my wife showing the difference between her and my mother in this area. If my mother saw the maid a little sick, she would ask her to sit down, would ask me to give her some medicine and would make her a cup of tea. She let her sit for a while and then start working. On the other hand my wife would ask her to start working and then give her some medicine. She would also ask her to make herself a cup of tea. In other words she was helpful but not eagerly helpful the way my mother was. When I made this kind of hypothetical incident-oriented statement my wife agreed with me and said that my mother and I were different from her in this respect. As time passed by she also started being more helpful—well, eagerly helpful.

I don't mind referring to an anecdote. It may sound trivial to some and not so trivial to others who take the suggestive significance into consideration. My mother told me not to go for haircuts on Thursdays because I was born on a Thursday. I followed the instructions very faithfully. On a Thursday, she asked me why I hadn't shaved and I said that it was she who asked me to not do it. She had a smile of satisfaction and said that she had only talked about haircuts not shaving and added, "nuvvuraa kodukuvante" (in Telugu which means 'son means, its you', roughly, 'you are the ideal son'). One can see how small things made her happy. She had absolutely no demands.

She said several things on different occasions which are worth remembering. She said that I should help people or keep quiet but I should not harm anyone. This has been my mother even in the case of people who harmed her. She advised me not to find fault with them because we would never know the circumstances that made them act that way.

Let's travel back to egalitarianism. The Bhagavad Gita has an interesting shloka, the 13th shloka of the Fourth Chapter. We will discuss this in detail because some people tend to associate Bhagavad Gita with the malady of caste division.

'cāturvarṇyam mayā: sṛṣṭam
guṇa karma vibhāgaśah.'

Sri Aurobindo renders the shloka as follows:

> "The four-fold order was created by me according to the divisions of quality and active function."

Sri Aurobindo takes this line of the Gita to be 'in fact an intellectual rendering of the well-known symbol in the Vedic Purusha-Sukta'.

HS Sinha in his 'Communism and Gita' (1978) makes a detailed study of the varna system:

> "The concept of the four-fold division of society (cātur-varna) is a much maligned one and considered not consistent with the norms of social justice. The Anasakti Yoga of the Gita, on the other hand, emphasizes its need on the basis of variety of guna and karma (153)."

By emphasizing on the guna-karma basis of the varnavya-vastha or the varna system, Sri Krishna is obviously negating something, viz. the Janma (birth) basis of the varna system. It is here we are actually illustrating the Buddhist theory of meaning, **apoha**. Here are some of the basic points of this theory as available in Ratnakirti's 'Apoha Siddhi' (Dhirendra Sharma (1969), Mouton & Co).

1. That which is envisaged as a positive entity also entails the exclusion of what is the other, and this is called…' the apprehension of negation' (differentiation).
2. By the term 'Differentiation' what is intended is not merely a positive entity (A); not merely exclusion of (the other) non-A, but the meaning of the term is the positive thing (A) qualified by the exclusion of the other (non-A).

Ratnakirti's view of Apoha can be summed up as follows: "Words mean something which at the same time is eliminated from what it is not—its negation from the rest the simultaneous."

In other words, **identification subsumes differentiation.**

In the shloka under discussion, when we assert that 'guna' and 'karma' form the basis of the varna system, we are actually negating or excluding the other phenomena like 'janma' (jati or birth) and 'dhanam' (wealth). This gets reinforced in a later chapter of the Gita (Chap 18: 41–44).

There is an important analysis of the semantic structure of the sentence that needs to be applied to our data to get correct interpretation.

A sentence, may be defined as *uddeśya vidheya bhavapanna padasamuhah* (a group of words related among themselves as the subject to the predicate).

Both Mimamsakas and Naiyayikas analysed a sentence into Uddeśya and Vidheya. Uddeśya contains a sense that is already existent and is known from other sources (siddha), while Vidheya consists of the meanings that are to be brought into existence (sadhya). Since vidheya represents 'new' information, the Mimamsakas hold that the tatparya of a sentence is found only in the vidheya portion. On the other hand Uddesya is 'something already secured by another means of knowledge'.

Let's now look at the line we have been discussing from this viewpoint.

Cāturvarṇyam maya sṛṣṭam, guṇa karma vibhāgaśa we can analyse this line in two different stages:

i.	Cāturvarṇyam uddesya	maya sṛṣṭam vidheya
ii.	Cāturvarṇyam mayasrstam uddesya	guṇa karma vibhagasah vidheya

In other words there is a nesting of uddesya-vidheya structure in this line.

The sentence is in passive voice (karmaṇivākya). The speaker is not speaking about himself. He is talking about 'cāturvarṇyam.' In a karmaṇivākya we talk about 'karma' and 'karta' or some other element will become 'mukhyaviseshya' (the primary modified).

Now I wish to show that to understand the real purport of the line under discussion, we need to take a syntactic view of this microtext in the context of the macrotext, viz. the Bhagavad Gita.

Let's start with the beginning of the dialogue between Sri Kṛshna and Arjuna, in the First Chapter, after the latter had a look at the two armies, with his chariot situated between them.

Shlokas	**Purport**	
Chapter 1	1. 28–30	physical disturbance
	2. 31–35	unwillingness to kill teachers, relatives and friends
	3. 36–40	sin of killing
	4. 41–44	dangers of varna-sankara
	5. 45–46	unwillingness to kill, willingness to be killed
Chapter 2	6. 4–5	repetition of (2)
	7. 6	uncertainty of the result
	8. 7–8	seeks guidance

Sri Kṛshna's reply to Arjuna starts in the Second Chapter.

Chapter 2	1. 2–3	condemns mental physical disturbance
	2. 11–30	futility of worrying about unmournables
	3. i. 31–38	sin of not doing one's duty; no sin in duty-bound system
	ii. 39–53	yogi; equanimity, sinlessness
	iii. 55–72	sthitaprajna, nishkama karma
Chapter 3	iv.	Karmayoga (detached action sinless action untainted action)

Chapter 4	v.	ancientness of knowledge
	vi.	Explanation of the super-self and the relationship between the self and super-self
	4. 13	all the four varnas are created by God and the decision is on the basis of their qualities and actions
	5. 14 onwards	karma, akarma, etc.

Only the 13th Shloka refers to 'varṇa,' not the shlokas coming before it or after it. If one observes the numbering I have given, Sri Kṛshna seems to have chosen a 'respectively-type' answer. He answered Arjuna point-by-point. The fourth point raised by Arjuna is 'varṇa-sankara', the hybridisation of varṇas,' assuming a birth-based, 'species-oriented' view of varṇa. Sri Kṛshna discusses it with a metatheoretical idea. Guna and karma decide the varṇa and equally importantly all are God's creation (maya sṛṣṭam). Then where is 'varṇa-sankara' and what is the fear about?

If one looks at Mahabharata in detail and raises varṇa-sankara it will be an act of atrocious logic. Raising it with Sri Kṛshna who is the 'Total Comprehender' (sarvajna) is inappropriate. Sri Krishna was a Yadava Prince. Who were Yadavas? The Yadavas descended from Yadu. Yadu was the son of Yayati, a Kshatriya king, and Devayani, the daughter of Sukracharya, a Brahmin, and the Guru of the Daitya Kings. Vasudeva, the father of Sri Krishna and Balarama, and Kunti, were children of Vṛṣṇi, who was a descendent of Yadu. If Yadu was the son of a Brahmin mother and Kshatriya father and no one had really called it an instance of varṇa-sankara, then what is Arjuna referring to? The Mahabharata is full of such marriages or 'coming-togethers' bearing forth valiant and famous children. An unbecoming fear expressed by Arjuna gets an appropriate dismissal from Sri Kṛshna.

The fact that the line referring to 'cāturvarna' in the Fourth Chapter, Thirteenth Shloka, neither before nor after, would have been a candidate to be rejected as an interpolation. But linking it syntactically with what has gone before, the shloka becomes a significant metastatement.

A scriptural text needs a super-specialist care both for interpretation and for translation. A given microtext has to be seen from syntactic (structure), semantic (meaning) and pragmatic (value) angles. While analysing a text we have to see what it negates or contrasts with, what its internal constituents are and what its structure signifies.

Let us close this lengthy discussion of varna in the mentioned shloka with the generalization that identification subsumes differentiation. The basis of a concept is said be a response or a readiness to respond in certain ways rather than others. Here the distinction is between 'certain ways' and 'others'. If one carefully observes the process of language acquisition in the case of children one would realize that they continually revise their 'systems' of differentiation. This is sometimes referred to as 'progressive differentiation.' In the Indian situation, we come across children who first use the same/only one word for 'cow' and 'buffalo'. Conceptualization-wise they are yet to distinguish between the two types of milch cattle, though they might use any one of the two words for the neutral concept. In course of time they acquire the 'distinction' as well as the relevant lexical items.

This leads us back to the Buddhist theory of meaning—the Apoha.

It is very important for us to ponder over the concept of 'non-A' (dissimilar instances). I wish to maintain that the 'non-A' phenomenon is a dynamic one.

	A		Non-A
(i)	cow	vs	tiger, wolf, etc.
(ii)	cow	vs	bull
(iii)	cow	vs	buffalo, goat, sheep
(iv)	cow	vs	calf

For an Englishman, the concept of 'non-cow' might not include a buffalo, but for an Indian it would. The horizon of 'non-A' will shrink or widen on the basis of the cultural contact or the immediate context of situation.

One may be wondering whether this lengthy academic discussion is a digression or the personal-memoirist information is the digression. Neither is. This is the instance of rambling realism, which integrates different strands of reality and they tend to float across. This kind of rambling is actually a stream of consciousness technique in a different form. No thinking man's life is independent of what he is intellectually. His social, physical and mental constituents constitute his integrated self. The integrated self of an individual gives us his cognizography when he starts explaining for others. And this text is engendered by my integrated self.

2

It was 1943, 24th of June. The village home was not small though the village was small. The village is named after a king called Teluguraya and the village is Telugurayapuram. This king had his capital in Podili, a town now in Prakasam district (Ongole). The time was 8:30 in the morning. The lady of the house cleaned up the forefront of the house while humming the song of *melukolupu*, a song asking Sri Kṛshna to wake up. At 8:30 a new baby boy woke up, delivered into this world by the daughter-in-law of the house. The lady of the house, the baby boy's paternal grandmother (PGM) was called Sridevamma and her husband was Venkataramanaiah. The name of the clan is Vennelakanti. That is used as surname of the family. It could be the adjectival form of Vennelakallu. But we are told a different story regarding this surname. It is said that on a New Moon day (amavasya) one of my forefathers, many generations ago, was credited with having got moonlight made available around. The king of the area is supposed to have said 'vennela' (moon light) 'kanti' ('ve seen). It is said that the king was pleased and granted Parikota a village near Kavali as a gift. The paternal grandfather was away on the day to Parikota to sell it. And his share of it, 25%, was used to clear off some loans. The PGF of the baby boy called him a lucky boy because he could clear off some loans.

Being an astrologer, the PGF attributed the luck of the baby boy to the Lagna of his birth: Karkataka (Cancer). Luckily by the western astrology also a Cancerian though with a bit of a hangover from Gemini. The Karkataka lagna with Brihaspathi/ Guru (Jupiter), Shukra (Venus) and Rahuvu and with Ketu in the Seventh House, Chandra (moon) in the Eighth House, Kuja (Mars) in the Ninth House, Śani (Saturn) and Budha (Mercury) in the Eleventh House and the Ravi (Sun) in the Twelfth House decided his fate and his luck. Interestingly these planetary positions take care of the diagnosis and the prognosis of a person's life. The baby boy's father later became a very knowledgeable astrologer and could foretell the events in this baby boy's life.

One may wonder how these planets influence our lives. Let's be clear about one thing. God is, let's assume, a reality. But God and divinity are subjective reality. On the other hand the planets and their rays are objective reality. Now comes the real problem: how can the planets, thousands of miles away from us, influence our lives? If we can link the ebb and tide of the sea with a distant moon it should not be impossible to link the distant planets with our lives. When a baby's head comes out, the unseen rays of the planet activate different parts of the cerebrum. The astrologer calculates the power and direction of the rays and links them with different parts of the brain which are responsible for different aspects of human nature. If one wants a foolproof solid support from biophysics, astrophysics and astrobiology to the relationship between planetary rays and human lives we may have to wait for some more time. But if we take the empirical proof given by the lives of different people we will not be unsafe scientifically. Dr Ramachandran gives us sufficient indication of the scientificity of astrology in his book 'The Tell Tale Brain'. The mother of the baby boy, Venkatalakshmamma, who we talked about in the previous section, always used to say in Telugu 'Buddhi (psyche) koddi (as per) Raata (fate)—Raata koddi Buddhi'. In other words, we can say the psyche and fate are dialectically related.

The baby boy is the author of this book which is a cognizography and an exercise in rambling realism. Right from 1965, my father had been predicting my future, and also the future of my wife, and later of my children, with unbeatable accuracy.

Born in 1943, I was lucky to witness the celebration of Independence. In 1947 on August 15th, I joined the school children to go to the house of Mr Jangam Reddy the President of Panchayat Board and he distributed sweets to the children.

Between the school and his place we raised slogans like Vandemataram, Swatantra Bharat Jindabad. I spent four years in that school—4th standard and 5th standard I completed in one year. Different teachers taught us different subjects and towards the end one Mr Krishnamurthy introduced me to English.

I remember one interesting thought that occurred to me those days. When someone said that Jawaharlal Nehru gave his speech in Hindi I surmised that in his mind he translated it from Telugu into Hindi. This is so because Telugu was the language of my being whereas Hindi and English were to be learnt. We can always say the languages we learn for different purposes are the languages of doing. But now I realise that for the language teachers, the languages they teach and work in and on are actually becoming the languages of their secondary being. When a language is primarily a language of doing and secondarily also the language of being, the user of the language should ensure accuracy, fluency, and propriety. When someone is presenting a paper at a seminar in English he/she has already promoted it to the status of language of secondary being. The people who go to English medium schools are actually doing injustice to the language of their being and end up with English as their being with lots of complications though. We do, however, come across cases where the children are allowed to strengthen their language of being too. The people who have strong language of being and strong language of doing become bilinguals with what is called diglossia, which refers to the situation where the two languages are equally efficiently used in different contexts though.

In 1952 I shifted to VR High School in Nellore. I was admitted to the second form (7th class) bypassing first form (6th class) after an entrance examination. Nellore being our district headquarters was a rich place, totally new to a village boy. I stayed along with my elder brother who was in the 3rd form (8th class) at the place of a puncle, V Srinivasarao who blended in himself strong love and a short temper. He was a very handsome and generous person. In Telugu my puncle is called chinnayana and in other dialects he is called babai. His wife, we called her pinnamma (younger to mother). Her name was Krishnaveni. She was so kind in feeding us and taking care of us in every sense. I can certainly say she was one of the founders of my positive thinking. In 1953 we shifted to CSS Government High School, Kullur about 15 km of walking distance from my village. My brother and I used to go to Kullur every Monday morning and come back every Saturday evening. We used to stay in a private accommodation and eat in a mess.

A strong foundation was laid for my growth in Telugu by our wonderful teacher Shri Darimadugu Kamaiah and an equally strong foundation was laid for my English by Shri Amancherla Adinarayana Rao. I finished my SSLC (eleventh class) when I was 14 years old in 1957. I was the shortest in the class and the English teacher used to call me Lilliput. I used to regularly participate in the elocution competitions in Telugu, English, and Hindi. This stint of four years in Kullur taught me lots of things. Caste differences shouldn't matter in public life. For the first time I heard the name of a community Bondili (Rajputs of Bundelkhand). We had a very good Maths teacher Mr Balaji Singh from that community. The main population of the village was mainly from a community called Balija (called Telaga, and Kapu in other areas). This was a very civilized community with total literacy. Emperor Srikrishnadevaraya's mother was from this community. Some of the people from this community were, in those days, bangle sellers who had their own secret language.

I passed out with good marks and stood second in the school. I also got 64 marks in English for which my teacher puncle gave me a gift of 64 rupees. But most important thing was that the one who stood first was one Mr Shaik Kalesha, who always stood first in examinations, elocutions, debates and essay writing competitions in Telugu, English, and Hindi.

This is an interesting example to show that brightness of an individual is independent of one's caste, religion and mother tongue. The basic genetic talent and hardwork decide our success. This is what Krishna said to his foster father Nanda at the age of seven when he was asking his father not to go in for Indrayajna. This is before lifting Mount Govardhan. He said the life of an individual is guided by his Nijaswabhava (basic nature) and his karma (actions including hard work). He added that Indra would not be able to change the fate of the individuals. Interestingly Krishna said this when he was seven, and seven is the age when we get to become conscious of our surroundings, fellow humans, and our place in the society.

It will be very appropriate to remember in this context that we had Telugu medium education till SSLC with a good base in English and some base in Hindi. For English we had prose and poetry lessons written by English authors. Similarly for our Telugu we had poetry by Kavitrayam, Tenali Ramalinga Kavi, prose by Paravasthu Chinnaya Suri and Rallapalli Ananthakrishna Sarma.

In 1957 June I joined the Pre-University course at VR College in Nellore with very interesting combination of subjects: Biological Sciences, Economics and Civics and World History, besides the compulsory English, Telugu and Human Achievement. It is for this last subject, we were asked to read a very good book: CEM Joad's 'The Story of Civilization'. The history subject was taught by a great teacher Mr Venkata Reddy and the textbook was by Sriharirao. Our botany teacher Mr Sitaramurthy was an extremely successful teacher though he was fast in his speech. We used to call him Circar Express for his speed and loved him for his teaching. Similarly our botany demonstrator Ms Padma Abraham, who handled our practicals, was a very good teacher. I still remember the definitions given by the botany lecturer for concepts like respiration and osmosis. Our Economics lecturer Mr C Mohanchandra Reddy was an excellent teacher and I remember many concepts of economics even today. The concept of employment generation even today guides my thinking about people and issues. For example I prefer labour-intensive industries to capital-intensive industries. Similarly the Malthusian theory of population is fresh in my memory regarding how population was controlled by several factors including wars. This also reminds me of the Kurukshetra War between the Kauravas and the Pandavas which is said to have been designed by the cosmic forces to reduce the population on the earth. I don't welcome mechanization which reduces employment. I finished my PUC with a B2 (second class subjects and applied for a seat in BA (Spl) with Economics, Political Science and History but I was given admission to BA (Spl) with English, Telugu and General Education as compulsory subjects and English Literature, Telugu Literature, Indian History & Modern European History as optionals. We had for our special English six papers of 100 marks each, for special Telugu two papers of 100 marks each and two papers of 100 marks each for History. We read Discovery of India (Jawaharlal Nehru) for our General Education. Our English programme both compulsory (two papers) and optional English (six papers) gave us a solid foundation of English language and literature. Durbha Ramamurthy who taught us Shakespeare as well as Cardinal Newman's 'The Idea of a University' (prose) could make us relish the beauty of literature. Paradise Lost was taught by Shri AT Srinivasarao and we appreciated the idea of the epic. V Ramachandrarao taught us prose and Malakonda Reddy taught us Modern Poetry.

Here I would like to own a misdemeanour on my part. Coming from a village I was not trained to recognise seniors and greet them. Mr Malakonda Reddy said to another teacher that my walking was offensive. He was right. I used to walk like Sivaji Ganeshan as the hero of folklore movies. Bad manners do not constitute acts of commission. These are more acts of omission because some people don't get to learn good manners as part of their growing up.

This BA (Spl) course gave us a strong foundation in Literary Criticism where we read original books written by Walter Peter, Matthew Arnold, Hudson and others besides the plays of Shakespeare, Christopher Marlowe and John Webster and poetry by Milton, Wordsworth, Keats and others.

Mr Vedam Venkataraman (VVR) was one teacher of English who influenced many students in those days. Even before the Central Institute of English was established in Hyderabad he used to teach us British pronunciation with the help of the English Pronouncing Dictionary of Daniel Jones. This really paved the way for my interest in phonetics and phonology. This was later strengthened by Madam Sudha Deshpande (Iyer) at Nagpur. Actually it was VVR who advised me to go to Nagpur University for my MA English because Prof Pothukuchi Subrahmanya Sastri was teaching there. My Telugu was strengthened by Poluri Hunumajjakiram Sarma, who was a great scholar of English literature, Telugu Literature, and Sanskrit Literature. The way he brought Valmiki Ramayana before us while teaching Dharmavaram Ramakrishnama Charyulu's Paduka Pattabhishekam is commendable. Similarly Darbha Venkata Krishnamurthy taught us Abhijnana Shakuntalam in Telugu by Kandukuri Veresalingam Panthulu. B Guruvareddy guided us with Duvvuri Ramireddy's Saraswata Vyasalu (literary essays). There were only 18 students in the whole University doing BA (Spl) with English as main optional, thirteen at our college and five at another college in Madanapalli. All of us finished our BA (Spl) with C grade which any way was not bad at that time and we were eligible for admission to MA programme.

Before I went to Nagpur I spent one year in the village in agriculture. This one year was not very eventful but useful. My mother used to give me fresh buffalo milk—a glassful—every day which I think strengthened my system. On the other hand walking under the hot sun most of the time without footwear made me very sensitive to sunlight sometimes even in December. I was prone to sunstroke which later I realised could be handled by taking Glonoine, a homeopathic medicine.

Here are my people: my parents, my brothers and my sisters. The one sitting next to my parents is my anna Prasadrao who took care of my second year MA programme. The blessing figure in the background is Bhagavan Ramana Maharshi, who sent my father back when he visited Arunachalam to become an ascetic. We were all born after that.

One fine afternoon my father came from another village with money borrowed from a money lender and asked me to go to Nagpur. This was in June 1962.

The next morning after having a rural breakfast of rice left over from the previous night and after taking a bag with a few clothes, I walked 5 km to reach the bus route. I boarded a bus to Nellore. I met a friend of mine there who took me to the railway station. I got a third class ticket to Nagpur by the Grand Trunk Express. Those days as reservation was not possible from villages, I never had a regular seat to sit on between Nellore and Nagpur. By the time I came to Vijayawada I felt hungry and bought a packet of rice without knowing it had non-veg curry pieces in it. I just had a bite when a handsome young man in the compartment looked at me and guessed that I was a vegetarian and said it had chicken in it. I threw away the rice but a piece already touched my teeth and for the next three days my teeth had funny feeling of pain. He helped me buy some vegetarian food and later he took me to a Telugu Reddy mess in Nagpur. He was a senior student in Nagpur University.

There in Nagpur I met Sri PVRK Prasad who had just finished his MA in English from the University. He guided me to file an application for my admission to my MA programme. Nagpur was the first city I ever saw. The Nagpur University library was very rich and in the same building we had the Post Graduate Teaching Department. I finished my MA in 1964 scoring just below 55%. Marks apart, I learnt a lot and I also earned due recognition from classmates, teachers, and others. I don't mind adding that I also earned some beautiful smiles and glances or maybe I stole them. This indeed was not because of my looks or grades but because of a small amount of charm engendered by Shukra (Venus) in my Karkataka lagna (Cancer ascendant).

Vidarbha is known for its hospitality. In terms of our Puranic history Sri Krishna's wife Rukmini belongs to Vidarbha. What really surprised me was the grading of hospitality given to even a visitor. The grading depends upon time and availability. A minimum of two things are offered to everyone: water and supari (betel nut). The next step is tea along with these two things. If time and availability permitted, tea would be preceded by a sweet and namkeen (savoury). I remember my father-in-law saying to me in Hyderabad that I was offering coffee or tea every time someone visited me. My reply was that I was a Nagpurian and I wouldn't forget what Vidarbha had taught me.

The food habits of Maharashtra are pretty worthy of emulation. A meal contains rice followed by roti and again closing with rice; dal, curry, dahi, achar, onions, lemons are part of the system. Sweets are for special occasion. I saw samosas for the first time in 1962 in Nagpur. One of the great delicacies was *patvadi* (also called *sambharvadi*), the main filling therein being coriander leaves. And the most popular sweet I knew was Shrikhand. Nagpur introduced me to homeopathy. I was feeling miserably weak, mainly caused by dream-wetting. My teacher Dr RN Roy who was a very successful teacher of philology and also a good scholar of GB Shaw was very kind to me. He was a student of the great scholar SC Sen Gupta whose 'The Art of Bernard Shaw' reads like a literary piece written by an Englishman. Dr Roy's 'The Philosophy of Bernard Shaw' and 'A Short History of the English Language' became very famous. I used to visit him quite often at home with my friend BS Roy. He took me to a homeopathy doctor by name Dr Karmakar for my weakness. There was a long queue. My teacher introduced himself to the doctor as a Bengali—"amiyo Bangla" and he replied "ashun" (come), "bashun" (sit). The doctor examined me and said the petrol pump was empty and he prescribed Acid Phos 30 for a month, and I was totally rebuilt. I can say it with full confidence that Acid Phos has been my tonic. I do take it occasionally even now.

In 1964 after I finished my MA (English), I was looking for a lectureship in English. I was selected by colleges in Gondia and Bhandara. But I wanted to stay in Nagpur. Dr Roy took me to Dr BR Ambedkar College of Arts and Commerce, which was just started on Deeksha Bhoomi—the place where Babasaheb Ambedkar embraced Buddhism. I was introduced to Principal YM Pathak by my teacher. I was interviewed the next day and I was taken in.

My tenure of two years at this college made a total change in my personality. From an average villager who took social differences as normal, I metamorphosed into a social being which demanded the treatment of fellow human beings as our equals. I would like to say with full understanding that Deeksha Bhoomi vibrated with wonderful ideas of Ambedkarism which exhorts us to seek knowledge to develop a spiralling sense of self where all are given the same opportunities as we seek for ourselves and to be genuinely secular and respect the rule of law. Thus I became a committed votary of Ambedkarism. After going through his writings and speeches published by the Government of Maharastra, I have come out with a small book: Dr BR Ambedkar the Jnanayogi (2016, Emesco). This spiralling self extends this concept to include others into it whereas the cacoonian self treats others as unrelated.

While at Dr Ambedkar College, I established 'Better English Association' to conduct special classes after the regular hours to improve the students' command of English. I used to give them handouts and help them with their pronunciation and grammar. We also published a small magazine on behalf of the Association and made it a part of college magazine (1965). Professor PS Sastri gave a wonderful write-up on the study of English for our magazine. His article explains why, what, and how to learn/teach English. Now we will look at how he guides us in this area. I will let him speak for himself to show the kind of English that the educated Indians of the time relished.

The Study of English (PS Shastri)

The national movement for freedom gradually crept into the educational field during the fifth decade of 20th century. Since then either politicians or educationists were busy conducting experiments on the young. First there was a move to introduce the regional languages as the media of instruction. The move is laudable and desirable. Ultimately the students have to be taught through the medium of the regional language. But the absence of a link language will tend to destroy the hard-won unity of the Country. This has led to an emphasis on the study of Hindi. A proficiency in the regional language and in Hindi may be enough for a large number of our Countrymen. But our Country has to advance. We need Science and Technology. We want to see the land self-sufficient in all spheres of life. Now the scientific and technological studies need a sound knowledge of the English language. A graduate in the Arts faculty may run away without knowing English: and he may not have to pay for it. But a graduate in the Science can't afford to be ignorant of English.

It was a matter of historical accident that out Country came into contact with England and retained it for more than a century. During this period we came to realize the meaning of certain ideals in the modern world: and this led to diverse activities. One such was to keep us in touch with what is happening outside our own Country. Today we are patriotic and yet we have come to believe in the basic unity of mankind. The world has grown smaller and more compact. No country can today stand aloof from the movements taking place elsewhere. Our refusal to study a non-Indian language of importance like English might as well isolate us intellectually, scientifically and economically.

In our vague talk about the need to retain English as a necessary foreign language, we seem to ignore one major factor. Throughout the ages, Indians alone have had the unique distinction of having an aptitude for languages. It is an aspect of the Indian genius to learn languages quickly and master them. It is not an exaggeration to say that we have in our country persons who can handle the language much better than many Englishmen can. In the first century when Apollonius came to India, his teachers of philosophy taught him through Greek. That is what Philostratus said in the second century. Our countrymen went to distant lands in the East and in the West and spread their culture and taught through the languages spoken there. We have to recognise this fact clearly. If we have a natural gift to learn languages easily, why should we try to smother it? It might prove a costly venture in the long run.

There are again persons who say that they want the English language, not English Literature. For the sake of argument, one may be able to distinguish thus. But one has only to think seriously for a while, then he would be convinced of the great error underlying this distinction. It is the literature of a country that best preserves the idiom of the language. The nuances of a language become clearer in the literature of that language. A poet like William Blake used vocabulary of about a thousand words in his songs; and not one word is out of ordinary usage. The ideas are profound and the vocabulary is limited, while an average Englishman has a vocabulary of about four thousand words, here is a poet satisfied with a quarter of that. A language like this comes to us in literature alone.

Moreover, our Countrymen have a general liking for poetry, not for prose. If we were to emphasise the language aspect, we would be strangling the real taste that alone enables us to learn a new language more easily. The English language as found in the English essays or in modern periodicals is not so simple as we are asked to believe by these champions of the language. Think for a while and remember what you learnt as a child. Some lines of verse will invariably come to the mind, not lines of prose.

Apart from these considerations there are other reasons too. Next to Greek literature, of all the literatures of Europe, it is only English which has a one long sustained cry to preserve the freedom and the integrity of the individuals. This is a valuable asset today in the context of differing political and economic ideologies. The demand to cherish the individuality of man is very timely today. Are we to be swallowed up by the absolutist state? The answer comes from the literature of England.

A great value embodied in English Literature is the need to cultivate sympathy and understanding. This was expressed by Shakespeare and the Elizabethans, by the Romantic writers, and by some in this century. The absence of sympathetic understanding breeds intolerance and converts a cold war into a hot one. This value may not have been present earlier in English Literature. But it became central since the influence of Greek Literature and thought came to be felt. Plato sought to replace force by persuasion; and TH Green preferred will to force. Gandhiji's concept of non-violence is Platonic; but it is Platonic as transformed by English Literature and thought. One can't get this value by studying the language. Those linguists unfortunately are out to banish poetry. Plato only wanted a kind of censorship.

Then again English Literature is rich in humour. It is not the coarse or vulgar humour, but one based on self-knowledge and sympathy. We may give up anything we like, but we can't give up humour. For here we find the fine art of living. It is the zest for living that has been absent for so long in our Country: and we have to foster it and tend it properly. The sense of humour that a Shakespeare or a Shaw could evoke in us is worth many languages and literatures. Here again it is necessary to state that this value too belongs to English literature.

There are many more valid reasons which compel us to read English language and literature. It is enough to state that only a good cause needs the efforts of people to persuade others to their way of thinking, feeling and seeing. Even in the bitterest days of our national struggle, Gandhiji detested English rule and not the Englishman or his language and literature. Let us preserve this great literature. For literature, in whatever languages it may be written, has no national frontier. Literature is the possession of man.

Is it not interesting that this write up of 1965 is valuable even today? Let's be guided by it.

Many people fail to make a distinction between script and language. For example the Roman alphabet is used to write English, German, Spanish, French and Italian. Devanagari is used to write Sanskrit, Marathi, and Hindi. There are cases where different scripts are used for the same language. For example Sindhi is written in the Perso-Arabic script as well as Devanagari script. Ki-Swahili is written in both Arabic script and Roman script. Keeping this in mind let's discuss certain aspects of alphabet.

Alphabet is the system of letters or signs used to commit a language to writing. This word, owing its form to the first two letters of Greek alphabet, alpha (α) and beta (β), has each character representing an individual sound. However by extension this term is also used to refer to other systems of writing which are not strictly alphabetic, i.e., do not have alpha and beta as the first two letters.

The oldest form of writing is said to be cuneiform composed of wedge-shaped strokes which were impressed with a stylus in cuneiform characters. This system of writing was mainly used in Babylonia, China, and ancient Central America and Mexico. The hieroglyphic style of writing representing a word, a syllable or a sound was mainly used by Mayas, the Aztecs, and Egyptians. A similar word-syllabic writing system was used in India during Indus Valley days.

After the Indus script which covers the history of writing in India from about 2500 BCE to 1500 BCE, it was during the period of the Mauryan King Ashoka the Great (272–323 BCE) that we see an extensive use of writing on stone. In the intervening period, though literature refers to writing, no specific inscriptions are available. So we cannot make any specific assumptions about the writing systems before the Ashokan era. The script used in the Ashokan edicts is called Mauryan Brahmi or Ashokan Brahmi. As for its origin, the script has been linked with the Greek Alphabet, the Phoenician (Aramaic), South-Semitic and North-Semitic scripts, Sanskrit-Tantric texts, whereas some other scholars talk of its Dravidian origins. According to a recent theory, the Ashokan-Brahmi script was the creation of the Buddhist monks. This script, essentially syllabic in character, is written from left to right as is the case with all the modern Indian scripts.

During the rule of Kshatrapas and the Kushanas the script underwent several developmental changes. More and more private individuals started using the writing system and better writing tools and techniques became available. For the first time a sharp-edged pen was introduced during the 1st century.

The next significant stage in the development of the script in India is found in the records of the Kings of the Gupta dynasty and their contemporary rulers from the 4th to 6th centuries and became the precursor to modern Indian scripts. This script is called the Gupta Script or Proto-Regional Script or Late Brahmi.

The post-Gupta era (6th to 10th century) witnessed variations in style and the script was called Siddhamatrika script. The siddhamatrika or the Early Nagari script was introduced into the western parts of the Deccan (Maharashtra) in about 8th century replacing the southern Telugu-Kannada script which was in vogue in those areas. From the 8th century this script developed into the Sarada script in Kashmir and Punjab, the Proto-Bengali or Gaudi in Bengali and Orissa. In Bengal the Gaudi script developed into what is now used to write Bengali and Assamese. In the 14th century the Oriya script replaced Gaudi in Orissa.

The Gurumukhi script used for Punjabi is found useful for typing because half letters are just a few. More importantly consonantal length is shown as a separate symbol, not doubling of a consonant.

In the southern parts of India the earliest script was the southern variety of Brahmi. From about 7th century three scripts emerged on the scene: (1) The Grantha Script (2) The Tamil Script and (3) the Vattelettu Script. The Grantha script was used to transcribe Sanskrit expressions and the Tamil script was used to represent Tamil expressions, especially in the northern parts of Tamil Nadu. Even within Tamil sentences, if a Sanskrit word appeared, the Grantha script was chosen; such mixed script was also called Grantha-Tamil script. The Vatteletttu script was used in southern parts of Tamil Nadu and also in Kerala. In certain areas Tamil script reflect only Tamil sounds whereas Grantha scripts have all the letters necessary to represent Sanskrit sounds. The modern Malayalam script developed out of the Grantha script during the 15th century.

Till the 15th century, Telugu and Kannada were written in the same script. Later the script diverged into two forms as they exist today. The earliest use of this script dates from the 4th century. It underwent significant developments between the 7th and the 10th century.

To sum up, all the scripts of India which are semi-syllabic or syllabic-alphabetic in character developed from the Ashokan Brahmi script of the 3rd century B.C.E. The Brahmi script is also the source for the scripts found in Sri Lanka, Burma, Cambodia, Indonesia, Thailand, and Laos.

Now back to Nagpur and me. My career underwent a real change thanks to Dr RN Roy. In the first week of July 1965, I visited the Department of English and met Dr Roy. He told me about a new programme the University was introducing and asked me to join the course. That was an evening course: Post Graduate Diploma in the Teaching of English. I pleaded my inability because I couldn't afford the fees right away. He literally held my ear with his fingers and dragged me to the office and made me fill the form. He paid the fees to be returned later. And this evening diploma shifted me from a pure literature stream to language and literature streams. Dr VR Kanadey and Dr Sudha Deshpande taught us phonetics and linguistics, and Dr PS Sastri taught us stylistics.

In 1966 I shifted to Hyderabad from Nagpur. After a four-month, very fruitful stint at Viveka Vardhini College as lecturer in English, I joined the Central Institute of English (later Central Institute of English and Foreign Languages, and now the English and Foreign Languages University) as a Research

Internee under the supervisory direction of Dr SK Verma, who ultimately chiselled my career and became my mentor.

I would like to make a serious statement here which we have already mentioned at the outset. My teachers, Dr Roy and Dr Verma treated students with love and concern on the basis of their work, not on the basis of their caste, religion and region, as I generally say on the basis of 3Cs: caste, creed and code. Code refers to the mother tongue of the student. I never heard them mention the word secularism for galleryying purpose but practised it comprehensively. I already mentioned how Dr Roy put me onto the language track by earring me to the diploma course which paved my way into getting general and applied linguistics. Professor Colin P Masica was responsible for my getting into CIE in 1996 where I was to do research under Dr Shivendra Kishore Verma. He did his PhD under the supervision Prof MAK Halliday at Edinburgh University and can be referred to as the first PhD in Hallidayan linguistics. He gave me a 15 page reading list containing articles and books in the area. It took me a full six months of intensive use of the CIE library which had journals and books donated by the British Council. After six months I approached him seeking permission to apply for a regular job of a lecturer in English advertised by Viveka Vardhini College. I also wanted his advice about my applying for admission to the Post Graduate Research Diploma in the Teaching of English at CIE. He advised me to apply for both but said the chances of my getting into PGRDTE were slim. I took his advice to apply for both and started working on my thesis: A Contrastive Analysis of Telugu and English Syntax. He corrected my chapters as if he was correcting a tenth class student's essay. He rightly said that the linguistic work should reflect scientific rigour.

In June 1967 I went back to him and told him that I had been selected for a lectureship at Viveka Vardhini College. He emphatically said, "No, you have to continue here." I responded saying that he had said my chances were slim. He said: "That was before I read your chapters." But I expressed my fear that later I might not get a lectureship anywhere in Hyderabad. His response reflected his nature. He asked me how much the salary was that I would get in Viveka Vardhini college. My answer was ₹ 275 per month. He said: "That kind of job I will get you anytime in Bihar but you have to continue here for now." This is how at every stage he took care of my career. I joined my PGRDTE course and continued doing research and at the end of the course, I submitted the thesis which I later revised as a book when I was lecturer in the Textbook Production Unit. Even here to become a lecturer in 1968 he had a definitive role to play.

The revised version of my thesis ended up as a different version thanks to the two-month course of lectures Halliday gave at the CIE in 1968. The Hallidayan model of linguistics continued the comprehensive tradition of linguistic theory started by JR Firth, who taught English at Lahore University and built into his theory ancient Indian ideas of linguistics. The Hallidayan model was originally called 'Scale and Category Theory' based on his article published in 1961, but richly influenced by his paper of 1957. But by the time he came to the CIE in 1968 the theory started being called Systemic Grammar based on his papers of 1967 and '68 in the Journal of Linguistics. That's why the revised version of my thesis ended up as a new version by incorporating new enriching ideas.

I might like to add here that Transformational Grammar was introduced into the CIE by Prof N Krishnaswami who had come back from Michigan. Krishnaswami introduced me to Indian Theories of Meaning by Kunjunniraja. This led me to prepare a 70 page monograph: Levels of Meaning—Their Linguistic and Pedagogical Relevance. Professor K Subrahmanyam introduced me to SK De's and Krishnachaitanya's works on Indian poetics which I used for my book on stylistics dealing with Dr C Narayana Reddy's poetry. In 1968 Professor Robert Lees of the University of

Illinois at Urbana Champaign visited the CIE and gave a course of lectures on Transformation Grammar covering its growth between 1957 and 1968. Now I will describe an incident and show how I would have proceeded had I been a practitioner of the theory. Later I developed a paper referring to this incident and the ideas I had in this regard. In 1968 when I compared the 1957 and 1965 models of Transformational Grammar of Chomsky, I thought that he should have gone one step further.

Chomsky (1957)

S → NP + VP

VP → Verb + NP

NP → T + N

T → the

N → man, ball, etc.

Verb → Aux + V

V → hit, take, walk, read etc.

Aux → C (M) (have + -en) (be+ -ing) (be+ -en)

M → will, can, may, shall, must

Chomsky (1965)

S → NP ∩ Aux ∩ VP

VP → V ∩ NP

NP → Det ∩ NP

Aux → Tense (Modal) (Perfect) (progressive)

The step I thought he should take was to be:

S → Aux + Lex

AUX was to stand for all the grammatical aspects of the sentence structure and LEX was to stand for all the lexical items of the sentence structure.

Prof Noam Chomsky visited CIEFL much later, in the early 90s. Here is Prof Chomsky with Prof SK Verma and others. The half-hidden faces are of Prof Amruthavalli and Prof Hemalatha Nagarajan. The other gentle man behind Prof Chomsky is Mr Ibrahim.

I casually mentioned to Professor Lees that Aux should be elevated further to give us 'Aux-Lex' model. It was in his office. Professor Lees looked up and down at me for a while as if he was sizing me up and said appreciatively, "I don't deny you for your originality, but this has already been done by Charles Fillmore". He then gave me the references:

1. Fillmore, CJ (1966) 'Towards a Modern Theory of Case'
   S → Mod – Aux – Prop
2. Fillmore, CJ (1968) 'The Case for Case'
   S → Modality + Proposition

Dr Michael Dobbyn was a Ford Foundation consultant at the CIE. I used to teach him Telugu. This made him recommend my name to the Peace Corps programme to teach Telugu to their volunteers. This helped me sharpen my ideas of teaching Telugu to English speakers. An interesting incident took place when I went to Delhi with some local officers to attend a national meet in Delhi. In the evening we had a dinner meet at the Oberoi Intercontinental. I was the only Indian in the group and all the other were Americans, one of them being a black. The Delhi officer remarked that Indians were funny because when you invited them to dinner they would come, eat, and go away. The officer who came from Washington DC exclaimed: "Can this happen among human beings?" I had to set the record straight. Well, it is quite possible I didn't soften my response. I looked at the American who claimed that he had done MA in Anthropology. To be honest I was not very polite. I said: "You said you did a MA in Anthropology from Paris. Haven't you read Linguistics across Cultures by Robert Lado? There he says Spanish bullfight is only as cruel as fishing. Same thing is here. If Indians want to meet and socialize they can meet each other any time. On the other hand invitation to dinner is for dinner and Indians believe in *atithi devo bhava*, i.e. "let the guest be your God." Well, they did nod their heads as if they agreed with me but they did not like my assertiveness. The black American later complimented me for my stand. This incident later put paid to my going to Texas to teach Telugu to the Peace Corps volunteers. Though the Hyderabad Office suggested my name to the Delhi Office, they objected to it saying that I was a cultural chauvinist. No regrets. I would not let anyone make illogical comments on India and Indians and get away with it.

Now let me come back to Dr Verma. He suggested my name to the Vice-Chancellor Meenakshi Sundharam (Madurai) to give a course of lectures at Summer Institute of Linguistics in 1969 on Semantic theories and language description. This was my first performance as a teacher of linguistics. 1969 summer I was asked by Dr Verma to apply for a Research Fellowship at the University of York, UK. On his recommendation I was admitted to the programme and a fellowship of £ 650 per annum was offered. The British Council agreed to pay my fee. When I calculated the cost of living at that time £ 650 was not enough to take my family with me to York. MWS De Silva, the Dean at the University of York was flying from Sri Lanka, his native country, to England via Hyderabad and Delhi. When he visited Hyderabad, several people told him that I would not be able to accept the fellowship and go to York. I met him for an hour. He interviewed me both academically and socially. After the interview, he agreed with the need to enhance my fellowship. He promised to see whether he could enhance the scholarship after going to York. He did. I got a letter saying that the fellowship was raised to £ 1100 per annum. This would in a sense take care of the expenditure of my whole family and also save enough money to pay for their travel. My own travel was to be borne by the University. Suddenly there was a small problem. I realised that my wife was pregnant again. So I expressed my apprehension about going to UK. Professor ML Tickoo said that England was a heaven for a pregnant woman. So he said I had all the more reason to go to England with the family. Professor Tickoo was a natural adviser. He once had said men should be grateful to their wives because it was the wives that make them fathers.

It would be appropriate for me to refer to what Dr Tickoo said in 1969. I used the word 'hate' for a leader. Professor Tickoo in his typical British style said: "Will someone tell him that hate is too strong a word to be used in this context." I suddenly remembered what Gautam Buddha said: right speech doesn't allow us to use words that hurt others. Similarly Jesus Christ very correctly said that what goes in (what we eat) doesn't defile us because it comes out the next morning. On the other hand what comes out of us as speech will defile us if it is not properly used.

I flew off to England in the first week of October 1969. My wife and children came to the UK by the end of December.

My father-in-law Amancherla Natarajan made all the arrangements for her departure for the UK. She came with our two children Gautam (born in 1967 June) and Sujatha (born in Nov. 1968) and the third one growing in her womb. To go to London to receive them, I rang up the York railway station to find out the train timings between 5 and 6 in the morning. With all the confidence ignorance (or limited knowledge) gives I said: "Could you please tell me the timings of some early morning trains to go to London?" He mentioned the timings of trains between 1 and 2 am. I said, trains between 5 and 6 am. "Didn't you say early morning trains?" That is when I realized for an Englishman morning starts early. Using expressions like early hours or wee hours of morning for him is the time between 1 and 3 am. Same applies to evening. For me late in the evening will be before nightfall and for the English man evening included several hours after sunset.

My wife was just nineteen and had her schooling up to only the 9th class but came all the way from Bombay to London without any doubt or fear. I saw her from a distance coming down the steps with full confidence. I received them with some woollen clothing for my children but my father-in-law had already organized the wardrobe for the winter.

It's very interesting to note that as there are caste restrictions in renting out houses in India, there are racial restrictions in renting houses in England. I did not feel hurt because similar things happened in India. I would not take-a-holier-than-thou attitude. The first three months, we were in a bedsitter of the York Housing Society. In those days Commonwealth citizens enjoyed certain social welfare privileges on par with British citizens. The main advantage was being part of National Health Service where by paying one pound per year we got free consultation service. As soon as we settled we registered with the doctor. Our doctor was Dr Letham. He advised my wife to consult the doctors at the antenatal clinic. They found out that she needed iron injections as an expectant mother. They gave me a choice: I could bring her to the clinic or they would send a nurse to give her injections at home. Naturally I opted for the latter. Next morning a head nurse came home with the iron injection. We just mentioned it to her that children as well as their mother had lice on their head and even on eyelashes which spread to me too. The nurse was shocked. She said: "Lice are contagious disease. Have you informed your doctor?" She enquired. I said I would but I think she did not take the risk and informed the doctor herself. The next morning by 8 O' clock the doctor visited us along with the health visitor. Medicine and shampoo were prescribed which could be procured from the shop, either free or at subsidized rates because it was free for children and the expecting mother. The York Housing Society came in the next morning and took away all our warm dresses, blankets, and mattresses for fumigation. By evening all the things were back and in no time the contagious disease was contained. We were asked to shift to some other place because the bedsitter was a small place. We finally got a single bedroom portion of a house owned by a Nigerian, Mr Samuel Aditaba. He was very helpful to us. We stayed in that house till March 1972. We grew potatoes, carrots and spinach in our kitchen garden. The British government gave one pint of milk at half price per child and a pint of milk free for the expecting mother. Besides, medicines were free for children up to 15 and for the expecting mother. In my case I would pay a fixed nominal price for the prescription. Besides, my wife was getting 27 shillings per week as family allowance. The third baby arrived on the 14th of April 1970 on the same day the great thinker Dr BR Ambedkar was born. When she was expected to go to the maternity hospital at Fullford the only thing we had to do was to call for the ambulance. I did not have to accompany her to hospital. I went and saw my wife and baby girl on the third day. My wife was all praise for the white staff nurses and doctors for taking special care of her because she was an outsider. They even got her pickles as part of her strictly vegetarian food. My landlord and his wife, who was actually a nurse in London, brought her back by their car. The concept of family attendant was not there and only visits by the family members were allowed.

My life in England was a great education strengthening my love for fellow human beings which was instilled by my mother. That's why I got naturally attracted to Jesus Christ's twin messages of **love** and **forgiveness**. When he says, 'love thy neighbour as thyself', Jesus Christ was recommending what I called the spiralling self in lieu of cocoonian self. In other words, when we love our enemies thus, there may be no more of them. When we forgive others' mistakes and hate only the sin but not the sinner, we are treating all as God's children. It will be blasphemous to say that God looks at us denominationally or in a sectarian manner. We need not hesitate to say that, assuming His omniscient, omnipotent, and omnipresent nature, He looks at all of us as His children, without any consideration for gender, community, race, caste and creed. Jesus Christ was right when he said the people who shout 'Oh Lord, Oh Lord' from the crossroads will not enter heaven but those who follow the path shown by God will enter heaven. The path constitutes love, forgiveness, compassion, dutifulness and socialness. Socialness refers to the ideas of equality, fraternity, justice, share and care attitude. It is this socialness which was in a sense contained in the ten commandments of the Old Testament and the Eight-fold Path of Gautam Buddha and also this constitutes the essence of the Holy Quran.

While in York I met many Africans, Europeans, Americans and South Asians. I had a friend from Pakistan whose name was Raja Shamshad-ur-Rehman. He used to visit us every alternative Sunday. He was working in a chocolate factory in York. Now comes the real relevance of the visit. My son was four years old when he referred to the Pakistani friend as Pakistani-Indian. I said that we were Indians and he was a Pakistani. My son said, "No, we are all Pakistani-Indians." He referred to American Indians who made a special sound by patting on their lips as Indians. We had only a black and white TV which made him realise the oneness of South Asian community. He referred to General Yahya Khan, Zulfikar Ali Bhutto, Shaik Mujeeb ur Rehman, Mrs Indira Gandhi and Mrs Bandaranayaka as 'our people', whereas Edward Heath, Herald Wilson as 'not our people'. Another interesting thing here was my friend was a Rajput and hence the prefix Raja. I commented that he was a Muslim and how we could call him Rajput. He laughed and said I was confused. He said: "I am Rajput by kaum (community) but a Muslim by mazhab (religion)." This should throw light on our thinking. We should not look for differences amongst people but look for commonalites.

Historically, South Asia and other non-English Commonwealth countries have English as their intra-national and international link language. One should not forget the fact English is not a foreign language like Chinese, Japanese, or Russian. It has been with us for long and if it is properly utilised as a link language it will not disturb the basic strength of our native languages. We have got to accept that we have in a sense nationalised this language from British Isles. That's why it can be called our ***National Foreign Language***.

Here let's survey language variation with reference to the contextual factors, and bring in the use of English in our lives.

The following contextual types can be postulated to handle the variation phenomena in language.

1. The context of 'area'
2. The context of 'class'
3. The context of 'subject'
4. The context of 'attitude'
5. The context of 'purpose'
6. The context of 'motive'
7. The context of 'contact'.

A speaker belongs to an 'area' (region). Speech varies from place to place. This variation may be in terms of just a few items or at the other extreme almost all the items. When we are very certain that the variations are in terms of only a few features, e.g., some lexical items, bound morphemes, etc., we may say this is only a matter of dialectal variation. At the other extreme we say that the languages vary. It is quite possible to find border-line cases in some places where we cannot be certain whether two forms of speech are two different dialects or two different languages. The 'areal' distance may not always correlate with the dialect-language variation phenomena. For example, the Jaffna Tamil and Tamil Nadu Tamil differ only dialectally though they are separated by sea. On the other hand Jaffna Tamil and Sinhalese are considered two different languages though they are 'areally' proximate. To explain this we have to bring in the phenomenon of migration. One can say with a fair amount of precision and correctness that dialect variation can be explained in terms of certain areas, e.g., Nellore Telugu, North Telengana Telugu, South Telengana Telugu, North Circar Telugu, South Circars Telugu, Rayalaseema Telugu, Hyderabad Telugu, etc. These varieties of a language are sometimes called 'geolects'.

A speaker belongs to a family which in turn belongs to a 'group' socially definable. This socially definable group may be a class or a caste. In terms of the label a speaker belongs to the particular group. When we account for language variation on this dimension, we can only speak of the tendencies, and not the actual membership. If we talk of three classes, A, B, and C in a speech community, we find many cases where speakers belonging to 'A', in terms of their social status, sharing the language features of the class 'B'. This depends upon the socio-economic and cultural background of the family. We can then speak of 'A-like', 'B-like' and 'C-like' varieties. The class-oriented speech variety is called 'sociolect'. These two contexts—'area' and 'class'—are parts of what has been called 'context of culture'. These contexts refer to the user—hence the definition of dialect (including sociolect) as 'user-oriented language variety'.

The contexts of 'subject' and 'attitude' can be considered parts of the 'context of situation'. The former deals with what we are talking about and the latter 'how we feel about it'. The variety decided by the subject is called 'register'. The dialectal variation may be found mainly in the case of intonational features, the grammatical forms, and lexical items in that order of importance. The sociolectal variation may be found in the case of segmental features, lexical items and also the grammatical forms. Registral variation on the other hand is mainly dependent on the use of lexical items belonging to certain semantic fields, on the specialized (technical) use of common words and the use of specialized expressions in the place of ordinary items. Let's take a few examples. 'Death' is expressed in Telugu in different ways depending upon the context of the subject:

1. *ca:vu:* day-to-day speech
2. *niraya:nam:* Buddhistic scriptures
3. *Sama:dhi* pondadam: regrading ascetics, etc.
4. *ma:rakam:* astrology.

The fourth expression is of special significance because when astrologers discuss this term they don't give it any emotive value which they give to the first expression. Similarly the expression 'parivartana' has at least three different meanings accountable in terms of the subject matter.

1. *Change:* day-to-day speech
2. *Rule-governed conversion:* linguistics
3. *Mutual exchange of houses:* astrology.

Register is usually defined as the 'use-oriented language variety'.

The context of attitude is of the speaker to the topic of the discourse or the hearer. It is here the distinctions of the following type are made: formal, informal, consultative, suggestive and matter-of-fact styles. For example:

1. *Matter-of-fact:* please take it away.
2. *Suggestive:* I think you should take it away.
3. *Consultative:* don't you think that we should take it away?
4. *Informal:* take it away/off, will you?

Though we have taken only syntactic variation for illustration above, stylistic variation may be in any of the linguistic features: phonology, lexicon, morphology and syntax. We can take the following examples for lexical variation:

1. (a) *bag:* informal
   (b) *win:* non-informal
2. (a) *fat:* pejorative
   (b) *chubby:* complimentary
3. (a) *adamant:* pejorative
   (b) *perseverant, zealous:* complimentary.

We have mentioned above that dialect and sociolect are 'user-oriented' language varieties and register and styles are 'use-oriented' varieties. Here the emphasis is on the choice of the proper code reflecting the speaker's attitude. These four types of variation—dialectal, sociolectal, registral and stylistic are discussed in detail by linguistis. The other three contexts are not usually brought in while discussing language variation. We have done it keeping in view their variation value.

The context of 'purpose' gives us 'language games', 'wordplay', 'hypercorrection', 'malapropism', and the like. Here, the participants in a speech act may be using language for entertainment, display of their 'superiority', etc. The language variation found in language games is predictably related to the 'normal' language. Let's take two language games Telugu children play 'ka-bha:sa' and 'nga-bha:sa'. In 'ka-bha:sa' they prefix 'ka' before every 'letter' (or letter complex).

Normal	ka bha:sa
me:ka (goat)	kame:kaka
kottu (shop)	kakokattu
palaka (slate)	kapakalakaka

In 'nga' bha:sa '-nga' is inserted after the first phonological syllable of every word:

Normal	-nga bha:sa
me:ka (goat)	menge:ka
kottu	kongottu
palaka	pangalaka

These language games are usually played by children as part of their verbal games. Sometimes children may use them with the 'motive' of 'secrecy' (see below). By 'word-play' we mean the use of words in a sentence for the sake of achieving alliteration, rhyme, etc. In the early stages of writing poetry some people indulge only in 'word-play' but not in writing 'poetry'. Some people in their attempts to show off their superiority in the handling of language may bring on archaic features, hypercorrections, difficult words, etc. All these constitute language variation in the context of 'purpose'.

Very closely connected with the context of purpose is the context of 'motive'. It is here we can bring in the feature of 'secrecy'. Here the variation is not as predictable as in the previous context. The secret language is a form of parasite language (PL) drawing on a base language (BL) The bangle sellers of Kullur (Nellore District, Andhra Pradesh) had a secret language based on Telugu. This they used among themselves when they didn't want to be understood by others.

For example:

Telugu (normal)	brahmadu	annam	tintunnadu
Kulluru bha:sha	ta:taga:du	pedam	cudtunna:du
	'The brahmin	rice	is eating'

a:dadi cu:pulu yedumu nila:lu
visurto:ndi ↔ nerusto:ndi
'The lady is looking (at us)'

We may say here that there is no difference between the two codes (BL and PL) as far as phonology and grammar are concerned. The only difference is the use of lexical items and with this the PL speakers achieve total secrecy.

The context of 'contact' brings us to bilingual or multilingual (or dialectal) situation. Here we can talk about diglossia, code-switching (code-mixing, also code-sliding), pidgin and creole phenomena. Diglossia keeps languages or dialects (linguistic/ dialectal diglossia) separate for well-defined functions. In code-switching the participants change their codes (again different languages or dialects). Pidgin, instant or institutionalized, gives us a new code drawing from two contact languages. Creole is further institutionalized as it completely replaces the use of the base languages. It is this context which gives us 'border' dialects which sound different from the inland dialects. The seven contexts we have dealt with account for the major types of language variation. To these, we can add a minor variation type:

(8) The context of muzziness (or choice).

Muzziness tells us that all the rules the child has created while acquiring his language remain available to him to some extent throughout his adult life. This accounts for the variation within a dialect. For example, in my dialect we use the following alternative pairs.

ayya:ḍu/ayina: ḍu, po:ya: ḍu/poyina: ḍu (also poyya: ḍu)
'became' 'went'

There is yet another minor context:

(9) The context of 'pathology'

This gives us cases where the speakers lose or do not acquire command of their speech due to some defect in their vocal apparatus or the functionisng of their brain.

We will now go back to English as our NFL. First we should treat all the languages spoken as the native languages of

Indian citizens as national languages. They may not all find a place in the Eighth Schedule, but most of them should, taking an objective criterion as the basis—say population figures. At present the following languages are included in the Eighth Schedule: Assamese, Bengali, Gujarati, Hindi, Kannada, Kashmiri, Malayalam, Marathi, Oriya, Punjabi, Sanskrit, Sindhi, Tamil, Telugu, Urdu, Manipuri, Nepali and Konkani. Sindhi, was added in 1967 and Manipuri, Konkani and Nepali have been added very recently. If say we take 70,000 as the minimal population figure to entitle a language for a place in the Eighth Schedule we will be able to accommodate many more languages in the Eighth Schedule. For example we can bring in Maithili, Bhojpuri, Avadhi, Adi, Ao, Bhili, Bodo, Dogri, Gondi, Halabi, Ho, Khandeshi, Kharri, Khasi, Khond, Kisan, Korkee, Koya, Kui, Kurukh, Lushai (Mizo), Ladakhi, Malto Munda, Mundari, Nissi, Santali, Savara, Sema, Tangkhul, Tripuri, and Tulu. This recognition helps the people feel totally one with this great land of rich variety. The fear that recognition of these languages will lead to demands for reorganisation of provinces is misplaced. The provincial boundaries are for the people and they have to be redrawn if they want them to be.

Once recognized, the Government can develop these languages on the lines mentioned above under the concept of language construction or development. This will be a positive programme which has very successfully been taken up by Central Institute of Indian Languages (Mysore). It does not matter if a given state has two or three language zones. Even if the areas with a great concentration of a 'minority language' are designed autonomous districts the given province stands to gain by way of serving the cause of its people. In many of these areas people tend to become bilinguals which adds to the national reservoir of human resources. Having a federal democratic set-up should yield us the happy result of letting each group grow to its best.

The Eighth Schedule should reflect the growing needs and aspirations of the people. It has Sanskrit and Urdu in it but

English is conveniently excluded. English is claimed by 232,875 speakers as their mother tongue in the 1981 census (published in 1987). Article 343 (3) of our Constitution provides for the continued use of English for all the official purposes of the Union. Article 348 specifies that English will be used in the Supreme Court and in the High Courts and for Acts, Bills, etc. Democracies should reflect realities, not impose ideals. However English need not be made compulsory for any kind of competitive examinations. If a good command of English is necessary for a given job, it can be imparted as part of training for the job. No particular language should be made compulsory for recruitment but one or two may be imparted as part of the training programme. The emphasis should be on any one of the Indian languages. The fear of national disintegration due to linguistic diversity is an avoidable myth.

The next point that needs to be considered is the imperative of identifying a National Link Language. Let us use two expressions here: Language of Wider Communication (LWC) and Language of Global Communication (LGC). The former refers to the use of language within a given country and the latter to the use of language between or among countries.

Different provinces in the country have their own official languages. The provincial governments can correspond with the Union Government in the language of their choice—Hindi, English or the Regional Language (RL). The Union Government, in its turn, can choose one of the three for communication purpose in consultation with the provinces. Here English, Hindi, and RL acquire the status of LWC.

Now comes the problem of the language to be used in the Union Government offices of different regions. At present the use of English continues to rule supreme in this context. The Union Government should establish regional zones parallel to provincial boundaries. The offices within the boundaries can do all their business in the regional language. Once they have reached the stage of corresponding with the higher office the correspondence could be in RL/Hindi/English. If private industry wants to stick to English as its LWC, if the people of the area want to continue the use of English in their area let them do it.

Next we can talk about the Language of Higher Education (LHE). As it is being done now a bit slowly, LHE status can be occupied by all the languages of the Eighth Schedule. It becomes imperative for the Union Government to take special care of languages like Sanskrit, Hindi, Urdu and English as they are pan-Indian.

When we come to the field of the international communication we have to consider two specific areas:

1. International correspondence and treaties
2. The use of language in the UN bodies.

Regarding the first area the language use seems to be on the following lines: correspondence between India and other countries is done in English. If a treaty is signed in India the language used mainly is English; but it would be followed by Hindi also. If the treaty is signed outside India, it shall be only in English. If the host county insists on their own language being used in addition to English their language is also used. In the case of second area it seems that English is being used exclusively.

We should adopt a practical and nationally sound policy of LGC. Whenever the official language of a country happens to be the same as one of the languages of India, then it should be the LGC between Indian and the other country. For example, we can use Tamil as the LGC with Sri Lanka and Singapore, Bengali with Bangladesh, Urdu with Pakistan and Nepali with Nepal. We can use Hindi with Fiji, Mauritius, etc. With regard to other countries we can give them the option to choose either Hindi or English as the LGC.

When it comes to the use of language in the UNO and other world bodies it is reasonable to expect a country of our size and population to be represented by a language which is not one of the five or six already accepted languages at the UN. Our representatives do use English at all levels of the UN. Besides this, we should go in for the recognition of Hindi as an international language which will be used at the UN. Even if this involves extra expenditure we should go in for this as a national symbol. One need not labour the point that Hindi would be a better candidate as our national symbol than English to be used in world forums.

The fact that English is a non-native language cautions us to make a special effort to develop proper command of the language. We have to choose the right areas to highlight in the spoken aspect of the language, the structural aspects of the language and the significant parts of the language. It will be right to see that the students of English are given proper training in the chosen areas. Let's now choose certain aspects of English and discuss them.

The command of a language is basically in two areas: **speech** and **writing.** In the context of English what we need is an adequate command of **Spoken English** (SE) and also of **Written English** (WE). When we know the correct **pronunciation** of a word we can use it correctly in SE. If we know the correct **spelling** of a word, we can use it in WE. The same is the case with the grammar of English. In SE, besides the correct pronunciation of words, we need to know the use of **intonation** in speech and conversation. In WE, we should know, besides the correct spellings, the use of **punctuation** marks. Sentence construction is common to both SE and WE. In SE however we come across shorter sentences and sometimes elliptical sentences as our intonation and gestures add to the meaning of the sentence. In WE sentences tend to be longer and more complex. We also use **italics, quotation marks and underlining devices** in WE.

Each language has its own grammar. For example 'a' 'an' and 'the' are articles which we have to be careful about.

We have to use **a** in 'A lion is a powerful animal'. We can't drop **a** in the sentence, 'a lion' in this sentence means 'any lion'. But when we say 'the lion' we are referring to the whole class or species. We don't use 'lion' (any countable noun) without 'a' or 'the'.

The is used before a noun to indicate specificity of reference. Between 'the' and the noun, we may have other items like numbers, adjectives and classifiers. For example, in 'the two beautiful college girls', college classifies the type of girls we are talking of—that's why it is called *classifier*. **Beautiful** is an adjective functioning as an attributive. When an adjective occurs before a noun it qualifies, it has an *attributive* function whereas when it occurs as part of the predicate as in 'she is beautiful', it is called a *predicative adjective*.

The, my, your (and other possessives), this, that, these, those are all referred to as determiners. In the structure of a noun phrase, only one of these determiners can occur. For example there was a Doordarshan programme several years ago with an unacceptable title 'This Our Land'. 'This' and 'our' being terms in a single system of 'determiners' cannot occur together; it should be 'This Land', 'Our Land' or 'This Land of Ours'.

Specificity indicated by 'the' may have different sources. If the source is in what has already been expressed we call it **anaphoric reference.** In certain constructions the specificity comes from something that comes later; for example: the resignation of the Chief Minister was expected. This kind of forward reference is called **cataphoric reference.** The specificity of the chief minister comes from the external context of situation. This kind of reference is called **exophoric reference.** When we say the earth, the sun, the moon the specificity is in the uniqueness of the object. This kind of reference is called **homophoric reference.** The definite article is also used with superlative expressions; for example: 'one of the tallest trees'.

The is always spelt the same way whereas we have two forms for the indefinite article **a** and **an. A** is used before words beginning with a consonant sound and **an** before words beginning with a vowel sound. For example: **a** university, **an** honestman. **U**, no doubt, is one of the five vowel letters (**a, e, i, o, u**) but in 'university' the pronunciation of **u** is yu: and **y** being a consonantal sound (also referred to as semi-vowel) the indefinite article has the form **a**; in honest, **h** is silent and the word therefore starts with a vowel sound: hence **an. The** also varies in pronunciation but spelling remains the same. The is pronounced with an **i** before a word beginning with a vowel sound (e.g. the egg/thi egg). But the vowel in **the** is pronounced the way **a** is pronounced in **about** before a word with a consonantal sound (e.g. the book/th-a book). However, when **the** is emphasised it is pronounced with an 'i:' (long i): he is the man for that kind of job.

Similarly prepositions play pivotal role in communicating with clarity and accuracy. In this area, **of** deserves special mention. **Of** is a preposition, but it has many different uses. Look at the use of **of** in the small text given below.

> She visited **the kingdom of Nepal** in 1976. She had an audience with **the King of Nepal.** She was asked to meet the **Director of Higher Education.** She met him. She had a **cup of coffee** at his office. They discussed **their plans of improving** the **study of English** in Nepal. **Of the thirty colleges** there were in Nepal she was to visit only a few colleges. She was given **a list of seven colleges** for her to visit. Unfortunately she lost the list given to her. She was given another **copy of it.** Now she visited **a number of colleges** given in the list and understood the **problems** otherwise she had just **heard of.**

Let's take out the phrases with **of** in the centre, or in the beginning or in the sentence final position.

The Kingdom **of** Nepal
the King **of** Nepal

the Director **of** Higher Education
a cup **of** coffee
their plans **of** improving
the Study **of** English
of the thirty colleges
a list **of** seven colleges
a copy **of** it
a number **of** colleges
problems… **of.**

In '**of** the thirty colleges…' **of** is more like a blend of 'about' and 'among'. There is no relationship intended with any other noun phrase. Similarly 'problems… heard of' is a different version of 'heard of problems.' Here also **of** is more like 'about'. In all other constructions, **of** comes between two nouns or noun phrases. No other preposition behaves like this.

Among the constructions 'N + of + N' also **of** behaves differently in different constructions. For example:

She wanted to see **the King** of Nepal.
But **he** was busy.

Here **he** refers only to **the king.** But in

He was given a cup of **coffee. It** was very sweet.

It refers to coffee.

In

The **Kingdom of Nepal**

of is equating 'Kingdom' and 'Nepal'. Similarly in

A list of **colleges**

we have difference of focus. We get a **list** (focus) but we visit **colleges** (focus). In 'a cup of coffee' the main element is coffee. When we want to pluralize it we say,

Two cups of coffee
Three cups of coffee

However it has now become common to say,

Two coffees for two cups of coffee.

Two sugars for two spoonfuls of sugar.

Here is another interesting behaviour of **of**:

I saw the **daughter** of the **King. They** resemble each other.

I wanted to talk to **her.** But for that I need **his** permission.

'her' refers to 'the daughter' 'they' refers to both the 'King' and 'daughter' and 'his' refers to 'the king'. That means in this construction both the elements (the daughter, the king) can be the main elements.

Have you noticed that there are three clear functions of 'of' in the sentences discussed above:

1. The second noun/noun phrase is **linked** to the first noun/ noun phrase (Kingdom of Nepal).
2. The first noun/noun phrase is **subordinated** to the second noun/noun phrase (a cup of coffee).
3. The second noun/NP phrase is subordinated to the first noun/noun phrase (the king of Nepal).

Both the nouns/noun phrases can be separately or jointly main elements.

I would like to present now different aspects of negative significance in languages. For the purpose of illustration I am going to draw upon English and Telugu.

Positive and Negative are terms of the system of polarity. But between these clear-cut terms, one might sometimes talk of positive-negative complex. For example:

Gr. Lex.

1.	I like him	(+P) (+P)	=	(+P)
2.	I don't like him	(+N) (+P)	=	(–P)
3.	I dislike him	(+N) (+P)	=	(+N)
4.	I don't dislike him	(+N) (+N)	=	(–N)

The system of polarity is found at different strata of language. To begin with we can talk of three major distinctions.

5. (a) Sub-sentential negation.
   (b) Sentential negation.
   (c) Supra-sentential negation.

Under sub-sentential negation we have:

6. (a) affixal negation.
   (b) lexical negation.
   (c) syntactic negation (specific or broad).

Affixal negation is the negation expressed by prefixes or suffixes:

7. (a) dislike (b) invariant.

Affixal negation is not possible for all the lexical items:

8. (a) love—*unlove (b) hate—*unhate.

9. (a) ista (like)—ayista (dislike) (in Telugu)
   (b) prema (love); dveṣa (hate); *aprema (*unlove).

Might be the more 'intensive' semantically a term is, the fewer the chances it has for affixal negation.

Affixal negation is syntactically positive (negation) whereas syntactic negation is negative. Syntactic negation is the negation where we use negative words like 'no', 'not', 'neither'... examine the following:

10. John dislikes Pammi, doesn't he?
11. John likes Pammi, doesn't he?
12. John doesn't like Pammi, does he?
13. John doesn't dislike Pammi, does he?

'Dis' no doubt negates 'like' but it does so positively whereas 'not' negates syntactically the 'assertion' of the item under its scope. Now look at the following:

14. John hates Pammi.

In words like 'hate', 'bad', 'dangerous' what we have is lexical negation. When a speaker has to choose from among three possibilities, 'dislike', '-not like' and 'hate'—he has to keep in mind the real intensity of his feelings as well as the pragmatic factors like contextual propriety. Any inappropriate use may attract labels like 'loose talk' and 'impulsive talk,' or 'lavish use of language'.

Besides specific negatives like 'no' and 'not' English also has what are called broad negatives which can be brought under syntactic negation:

15. Hardly
    Scarcely
    Barely
    Seldom.
16. She hardly resembles her mother, does she?

The most common antonymous pair of expressions like

17. Works hard
18. Hardly works.

Has a fairly parallel creative pair in Telugu:

19. (T) kastapadipaniceyu 'hard' 'work' (work hard).
20. (T) kastammida paniceyu
    'hard on' 'work'
    (hardly works).

We have already mentioned that words like hate, bad, dangerous illustrate lexical negation. But there are also cases where a word may be negative in certain referential contexts and positive in certain other contexts. For example, 'slim' and 'thin' are taken to be 'positive', 'negative', in their implications. In an expression like 'slim chance' it may turn out to be 'negative'. But in 'thin paper just right for a letter pad'; 'thin' will be 'positive'. Similarly in 'thick lips' and 'thick binding' the implications differ. 'Thick lips' may not necessarily have the same implication for all ethnic groups and for all cultures.

So far we have talked about affixal, lexical, broad, syntactic and specific syntactic negation. All these come under what I called sub-sentential negation. Now let's look at what I wish to refer to as sentential or propositional negation. Examine the following:

21. (E) Why will he do it?
    (implication: He won't do it)
    (T) atanuendukucestāḍu?
    He why will do
    (implication: atanuceyyaḍu)
    He won't do

22. (a) atanu maaintiki vacci calarojul ayindi
    he having come to our home many days passed.
    (b) Atanu ma intiki raka calarojul ayindi
    he to our home not having come many days passed.

In (21) an interrogative expression is used to make a negative statement with certain attitudes attendant on it. In (22) an interesting grammatical phenomenon is present: 'vacci' 'raka' are antonymous. But at the level of sentence the effect is the same:

(c) atanu cala rojuluga maa intiki raledu
    he many days for our house to not come

This possibility however is not available with all the verbs. Moreover [22(a)] has another meaning too:

23. He came here many days ago (he is still here).
    which is again the opposite of [22(c)]. Also look at:

24. atanu ceptegada ne ceyyaḍāniki ?
    he told if (only then) I doing for
    has two negative statements in it:
    (a) he didn't tell me—atanuceppaledu
    (he didn't tell)

(b) I didn't do it—ne ceyyaledu
(I didn't do)

Besides, [24(a)] is shown as the cause and [24(b)] as the effect. Rhetorically expressed, it has no overt negative marker, but the negation of both the propositions is very clear. In these cases what we see is the negative intentional base but the expression has no overt negation and the structure is transparent enough for negative inference.

Supra-sentential negative is discoursal negation. This can be treated under two headings—(a) cotextual and (b) contextual. Co-textual negation is a sort of delayed negation. If the negative feelings are expressed in irony and the real significance becomes clear at a later stage we can call it cotextual negation. In Shakespeare's Julius Caesar, Mark Antony's funeral oration where Brutus and others are referred to as 'honourable men' and the later parts of oration make it clear that he doesn't mean it, one will have to reinterpret the first part of the text in the context of the later part.

'Contextual negation' is what we get in the cases where the beliefs and expectations of an individual or a community are involved. Let us examine the following:

25. (a) Once upon a time there was a king
    (b) i. But he was a good king
        ii. But he was not a good king
        iii. But he was a bad king
        iv. But he was not a bad king
26. (a) Once upon a time there was a rakshas (demon).
    (b) i. But he was a good rakshas
        ii. But he was not a good rakshas
        iii. But he was a bad rakshas
        iv. But he was not a bad rakshas

The appropriate choice from among the second sets of sentences depends upon the cultural image we have of a king or a rakshas. The negative or positive values attached to entities and issues in such cases are pragmatic.

In English, when we want to add extra information, we use **intensifiers, adjectives** and **adverbs.** One can clearly notice the basic adverbial nature of the word even when it is used as an adjective. Fast work is 'work which gets done fast' and 'a fast horse' is a horse that 'runs fast'. When '—ly' is added to adjectives we get adverbs, e.g., beautiful—beautifully; frank—frankly. But when '—ly' is added to nouns we get adjectives, e.g., man—manly; cost—costly. Expressions like 'very' are also called adverbs by some grammarians. Actually they are intensifiers used to modify adjectives or adverbs to intensify their meaning, e.g., **very good**; **very frankly**. Adjectives and adverbs are used for modification. Because intensifiers are used to qualify the modifiers they are also called submodifiers.

When we appreciate someone or something we use the word 'compliment' for what we have done. **Compliment** indicates 'praise', 'admiration' or 'respect' as in 'he complimented Mohan for handling the situation so well'. The word **compliments** is used to express good wishes or respect in a formal situation. If we give or send something to someone **with our compliments**, we mean that we are sending it to them free. In none of these contexts can we think of **best compliments. With compliments from** or **with the compliments of** or **with my/our compliments** are all acceptable but not the most frequently used **with best compliments.**

Let's now talk about the elements of speech. When we utter words we use **consonants** and **vowels**. Some vowels and consonants need special attention. This discussion reflects 'me' and crops up in my conversation with people who raise points of English pronunciation.

A, e, i, o, u are referred to as vowel letters—each one of them has at least two principal pronunciations. The **a** in glad, cap, shadow, family has what is generally called open palatal vowel sound. Generally dictionaries use the symbol **æ** for this pronunciation. But in make, able, navy, change, hate, favour **a** is pronounced as a simple long vowel **e** in Indian English but in native dialects it is pronounced as a complex vowel 'ei'. If we treat the former as **short** pronunciation **æ** and the latter as **long** pronunciation ei we can generalize their occurrence as follows. The short pronunciation occurs in single-syllable words ending in one or more consonants and in such **two-syllable** and **polysyllable** words where the stress is on the syllable and the words end in one or more consonants, e.g., glad, catch, canal, adapt, attack, compact, contact, dash, mass. This pronunciation occurs also if there is a final silent 'e' after two or three consonants in a word, e.g., badge, handle, angle, cattle.

If the stress is on the **pre-final syllable** with 'a' in it, short pronunciation occurs, e.g., candy, valley, expansion, fantastic, attitude, ambassador. In **polysyllabic** words in which the main stress is on the third or fourth syllable from the end 'a' is pronounced [æ]; agony, animal, average, calendar, camera, fabulous, family, gratitude, academy, calamity, vocabulary.

The long pronunciation **ei** is found when 'a' is followed by a consonant plus **silent e:** make, name, efface, parade, female, imitate. When we find an I or r before silent **e,** the same long pronunciation is heard: able, acre, sabre, April, hatred, sacred. In words where the stressed 'a' is followed by another pronounced vowel the pronunciation is 'long'; archaic, prosaic, chaos, laity. When in a word, a stressed syllable with **a** is followed by an unstressed ending containing one of the combinations ia, io, iou, ea, eo, eou, eu, ie, the pronunciation of 'a' is 'ei'; nation, occasion, contagion, palatial, audacious, spacious, courageous, patient, labial, Australian, radiant, mania, radio.

Besides these two pronunciations—[æ] [ei], 'a' is also found to be pronounced in a large number of words as [a:]. This we find when a occurs before '-ff', '-ft' and '-ph' in word final position, e.g., chaff, staff, after, craft, graft, raft, rafter, shaft. In some cases both [a:] and [æ] are heard: photograph, autograph, paragraph: interestingly 'graph' is pronounced [græf] with [gra:f] as an alternative pronunciation. But in 'photograph' the first choice is [gra.f] and [græf] is only an alternative. In 'photograph' the stress is on **pho**. It looks as though in these words where 'a' is **primarily stressed** it is [æ] but when it has **secondary stress** it is [a:]. 'A' when it occurs in unstressed syllables it is not [æ][a:] or [ei], but only a short 'i' or a neutral vowel, generally shown as [ə] as in 'about'. In 'photography' where the stress is on '-to-', third syllable from the right, 'gra' is pronounced [grə-], and 'pho- is pronounced [fə].

A is pronounced [a:] before '-nce', '-nch', '-nd', '-nt': advance, chance, dance, enhance, glance, lance, Chancellor, blanch, branch, command, demand, chant, plant, slant, can't, shan't, also example, answer, sample. In certain words there is a variation possible between [æ] and /a:/; askance, stance, ranch, transform. But in the following words generally [æ] is heard: finance, romance, cancel, bland, grand, random, pant, cant.

Words where we have –sk, -sp, -ss, -st, -th, after 'a' the pronunciation is [a:]:ask, bask, cask, flask, mask, task, basket, casket, rascal, clasp, gasp, raspberry [ra.zbrl], grass, pass, pastime, cast, caste, castle, disaster, mast, last, master, pasture, plaster, repast, vast, flabbergast, bath, father, rather.

Variation between [æ] and [a:] is heard in Basque, bask, exasperate, masculine, mass, bastard, dastard.

R as a letter has special significance for dialectal variation in English. General American, Irish, Scottish, Cornish, and Indian dialects of English are generally referred to as 'r-dialects'. These are the dialects where 'r' is pronounced wherever it may be, though the quality may be different. In Standard British English—generally referred to as Received Pronunciation—'r' is not pronounced when the following sound is a consonant, e.g., part, warehouse, car rally. It is pronounced when the following sound is a vowel, e.g., rate, pair of scissors. Some British speakers bring in 'r' when a vowel-final word is followed by a vowel-initial word, e.g., India (r) and China. Here 'r' is called intrusive 'r'. We need not follow this at all.

A has long pronunciation (a:), when it is followed by 'r' and when it is not followed by any other vowel letter, e.g., car, scar, star, farm, hard, market. If 'r' is followed by a silent 'e' or another consonant followed by a silent 'e', 'a' is pronounced differently, e.g., care, scare, stare, scare. If 'a' is preceded by w, qu, the pronunciation is 'labialised'—swarm, war, warm, wharf, quart, quarter. The pronunciation of 'a' in 'are' seems to totally ignore the presence of 'e' whereas in 'area' 'e' is not only deciding the quality of first 'a' but has its own presence (i) too. In words like baron, tariff, a is pronounced as in cap. In harass the two 'a's are differently pronounced. The first one is part of a stressed syllable and has the same pronunciation as 'a' in 'cat'. The second 'a' is part of an unstressed syllable and so has a very short pronunciation as in 'about'.

E has two pronunciations—short (as in bet) and long (as in be). The long pronunciation is longer than 'i' of 'bit'. In **monosyllabic** words ending in one or more consonants and in **disyllabic or polysyllabic** words with stress on the last syllable and ending in one or more consonants 'e' has short pronunciation, e.g., peg, test, fell, mess, contempt, resurrect. If the word has a final silent 'e' the pronunciation is short too: else, sense, fence, twelve, hedge. If the stress is on the pre-final syllable in disyllabic or polysyllabic words, 'e' has short pronunciation: fellow, member, apprentice, domestic, meddle, tremble, wrestle, centre, scepter, spectre. But in metre 'e' has long pronunciation (i:) but it becomes short (e) in metric. Short pronunciation is found also in the cases where the stress is on third or fourth syllable from the end: democrat, edifice, enemy, genuine, legacy, pedigree, decorative. In 'extreme' the second 'e' has long pronunciation, but in extremity, 'e' has short pronunciation. Similarly, 'e' in compete has long pronunciation but in competitor and competitive it has short pronunciation. In both the cases the syllable with 'e' is stressed and the short pronunciation is heard when it is followed by two or more syllables.

E has long pronunciation in words where it is followed by a single consonant (+l/r) plus silent 'e', e.g., cede, eke, scene, theme, extreme, intervene, complete, centipede, concrete, cathedral. This pronunciation is also found when 'e' is in the final position or before another vowel: he, she, he, we, me, neon, peon. Where e is followed by a single consonant plus unstressed ending containing any one of the combinations ia, io, ion, ice, ea, eo, eon, ea, ie and -ive, it has long pronunciation:

> completion, cohesion, legion, allegiance, venetian, facetious, specious, genial, comedian, lenient, medium, adhesive, also in legal, lethal, venal.

E in combination with 'r' gives us different pronunciations. In clerk, sergeant, Derby the vowel sound is (a:) (as 'a' in father), in interfere, severe, sincere, 'er' with silent 'e' gives us a two-vowel pronunciation: (iə) When 'r' is part of the following syllable 'e' has short pronunciation: cherish, perish, inherent, merit, peril, very, experiment, heroine, severity, clerical, spherical, berry, errand, error, herring.

Alex Wijk's rules of the pronunciation for the English Language (Oxford University Press, 1966) is an excellent guide in this regard.

Let's now discuss i (y) o and u. These letters also have short and long pronunciation. The short pronunciation of i (i) is found in big, finger, pit, wind, (N), chit; the long pronunciation [ai] in dry, fine, fibre, vital, kind, wind (v), mind. The short pronunciation of 'o' is found in drop, follow, modest, shop, cop, fox; the long pronunciation is found in go, home, noble, old, roll. The short pronunciation of 'u' is found in much, hundred, cut, public, putt; the long pronunciation (ju:) is found in duke, music, unity, use. We should remember here that 'short' and 'long' pronunciations are of totally different qualities. We have adopted these terms for the sake of identity and reference.

The short pronunciation of these vowel letters—i (y), o, u—as in the case of 'a' and 'e' is found in **monosyllabic** words ending in one or more consonants and in such **disyllabic or polysyllabic** words with stress on the last syllable and end in one or more consonants, e.g., sit, pit, shit, kiss, miss, myth, hymn, cyst, rob, fond, cross, allot, cost, cup, much, dull, fuss, deduct, conduct, shun, fun, fund, bridge, rinse, response, involve, pulse, plunge.

Short pronunciation occurs also in **disyllabic or polysyllabic** words where the stress falls on pre-final syllable and the stressed vowel is followed by two or more consonants: kitchen, picture, little, simple, whistle, system, syllable, sympathy, doctor, hospital, opposite, longitude, bottle, fondle, jostle, hunger, function, redundant, rustic, custody, uncle, muscle, struggle. But in words like Bible, noble, cyclone, nuclear, hybrid, the letters have long pronunciation.

In **polysyllabic** words in which the main stress falls on the third or fourth syllable from the end, 'i' (y) and 'o' have short pronunciation and 'u' pronunciation, e.g., cinema, citizen, cylinder, liberty, frivolous, vinegar, predicament, solicitor, pacific, political, typical, botany, colony, dominate, opera, policy, poverty, prosecute, apology, hippopotamus, ironic, symbolic. As mentioned above, 'u' has long pronunciation: cucumber, fugitive, funeral, mutiny, musical, cubic, Munich.

Now **i** (**y**), **o** and **u** have long pronunciation in words where the vowel is followed by a consonant plus silent 'e': life, fine, type, rhyme; joke, hole, hope, rope, cube, amuse, presume. We do find however numerous exceptions to this general observation. In the case of 'i' we also get long [i:], instead of [ai] as in machine, magazine, routine, intrigue, antique, unique. We have short pronunciation of **u** in words with **o** as in come, some, done, none, one, above, dove, glove, love. Please note 'monk' is also pronounced as if it was spelt 'munk'. **o** has long [u:] pronunciation in move, prove, approve, improve, reprove, lose, whose.

In words where the vowel letter is followed by a consonant plus 'I' or '**r**' and **silent 'e'** we get long pronunciation: Bible, idle, rifle, disciple, title, cycle, fibre, library, cypress, noble, cobra, appropriate, bugle, scruple, duplicate, lucrative.

In 'give' we have short pronunciation of 'i'. The same is the case with 'live' when it is a verb but we have long pronunciation [ai] when it an adjective. Similarly 'wind′ (N) has short pronunciation but 'wind′ (verb) has long pronunciation. In bind, child, wild, **i** is long but it is short in hindrance, children, wilderness.

As we have seen in the case of **a** and **e**, the presence of r after **i, o and u** will give us different pronunciation. For example, in fir, virtue, stir, bird, we have a pronunciation which is slightly longer than 'a' in 'about' and 'alone' but less open than the vowel sound heard in come, cut and shut. In fire, iron, desire, lyre we have what some scholars call a triphthongal sound—a sound with three vowel qualities. When 'r' is part of the next syllable i (y) is short: miracle, spirit, lyric.

In word, world, work, worm, 'or' is pronounced as 'ir' in first. In worsted and Worcester we have simple 'u' as in 'put'. Please note 'Worcester' has only two syllables: 'wuster'. The last syllable is similar to 'er' in 'worker'. In cur, fur, occur, concur, church and murder, 'ur' is like 'ir' in'first' and 'or' in followed by 'u' and the short vowel heard in 'alone' (juə).

The letters **c** and **g** have a history. They represent two sounds each—k, s, g, j. [k] is heard when **c** is followed by **a, o, u** or a consonant, and syllable finally. Similarly [g] is heard when **g** is followed by **a, o, u** or a consonant and also syllable finally. Before **e, i,** and **y, c** is [s] and **g** is [j]. Dictionaries use the symbol [dʒ] for /j/. **C** is [k] in cat, cold, cup, cry, act, music. C is [s] in cell, city, cycle; 'celtic' has both [k] and [s] pronunciations. [Keltic] is the general usage whereas [seltic] is the name of the football team. The word cymru (referring to the Welsh people or language) starts with [k]. In its plural form foci c is [s]; however some people retain [k] of the singular [-sai/-kai:], **g** is [g] in gain, go, gun, beggar, glad, great, pigment, egg, etc. In a few words however we hear the [j] sound though the general rule expects [g]: margarine, gaol (same as jail), mortgagor, Reg, Veg. The last two words retain the [j] of the full words: Reginald, Vegetarian.

There are a few words where 'g' is [g] before 'i', 'e', 'y', e.g., gear, get, give, gynaecology, gertrude, tiger, bogie. In hegemony we hear [j] or [g]. In 'pedagogue' the final consonant is [g]. But in pedagogic and pedagogy the second 'g' could be either [j] or [g]. In Reggie, exaggerate and suggest we hear [j]. Otherwise in all the words where we have '-gg-' the sound is [g]: dagger, nugget, sluggish. It is interesting to note that '-cc-' gives us different pronunciations. In occupy, succour, succumb, and tobacco, 'cc' is [k]. In *accident, accent* and *success*, 'cc' is [ks]. Similarly 'sc' reflects different pronunciations. In *scare, discuss* and *disc* 'sc' is [sk] but in *scene, scent, science, crescent,* and *scythe* it is [s].

Ch is [ch] in words like chalk, chance, bench, branch, belch. But ch is [sh] in champagne, charlotte, chassis, chauffeur, chef, attache, cliché, chiffon, brochure, parachute, niche (ch is also heard in this word). In crèche **ch** is [sh], not [ch]. In Greek loan words 'ch' is [k] chlorine, Christ, chromosome, cholesterol. Cholesterol is combination of chole (bile), stereos (solid) and '-ol' [a suffix]. Cholesterol is found in all cells of the body and it helps to carry fats, produce oil for the skin and hair, and make hormones. The presence of an abnormal amount of cholesterol in the blood is called cholesterolemia or cholesteremia. Homeopaths use cholesetrinum, a remedy made from gall-stone (a stone from the gall bladder), to cure several ailments of the liver and also to bring down the level of cholesterol in the blood.

Ch is also [j] is some words: spinach, sandwich, Greenwich. Alternatively we hear [ch] in these words.

G is [j] in words like gem, gesture, gibe [jaib], gist, gypsum, refrigerator, gorgeour magi (also –g-), fragile, Niger, Nigeria. **G** is pronounced [ʒ] [as 's' in measure, pleasure and treasure] in barrage, garage (also 'j'), regime, genre.

Gh is [g] in ghost, yoghurt, ghetto. It is [f] in laugh, draught, enough, Hougham. Hougham is a place in Kent (in England) and is pronounced with [f] as the medial consonant. In this word **ou** is pronounced as **u** in cup and **a** is a short vowel as **a** in around. In hough **gh** is pronounced [k]. Hough (proper name) is pronounced with [f] '-Burgh' to represent 'borough' as in Edinburgh gives us a short vowel sound. Hamburg has a final [g] and refers to 'a small variety of the domestic fowl'.

The pronunciation of a sound is bound to be affected by its environment. This is more so in the case of consonants. Let's look at the way the past tense (and past participle) suffix is pronounced. In walked, ranked, placed, hoped, **d** is pronounced (t), because the preceding consonants k, s, p are voiceless; in bagged, raised, robbed, (g), (z), (b), are voiced consonants and the past tense marker is pronounced (d). If it comes after 't' or 'd' it is pronounced (id), e.g., wanted, boarded, slated. If the preceding sound is a vowel or a nasal the pronunciation is (d), e.g., applied, overawed, donned, rammed.

A similar principle operates in the pronunciation of **s** used as third person singular marker in the case of verbs (thinks, sings, praises), plural marker in the case of nouns (sticks, bags, roses), possessive marker (Mary's, Herbert's, John's) or as reduced form of is (e.g. Peter's not coming home tomorrow). If **s** is preceded by (s), (z), (ch), (j), (sh) it is pronounced (iz), e.g., kisses, churches, praises, judges, bushes rashes, garages, mirages. If s is preceded by (p), (t), (k) it is pronounced (s): weeps, beeps, cats, acts, licks, Nick's, makes, hates. When 's' is preceded by (b), (d), (g), nasals, or vowels, it is pronounced (z), e.g., cabs, gods, dogs, pens, lambs, kings, bananas, trees, Andy's, goes, comes, runs...'House' has a final (s) and 'houses' is pronounced with two (z)s. (hauziz).

S as part of a word also shows variation in pronunciation. In the beginning of a word it is always (s); sit, seat, set, sat, sort, sought, soot, so, said, sight, stale, scare, snore, small, spoke. But in sure, sugar it is pronounced (sh). In the word final position 'ѕ' is generally (s), (but not always): gas, bus, canvas, alas, us. In several words we find -ss in word final position giving us (s): Compass, embarrass, goodness. In the following words 's' is pronounced (z): as, has, is, was, his, lens, James, Wales, Mars.

In axis, crisis, diagnosis, thesis, the final consonant is (s) and the preceding vowel (i). But in the plural counterpart of these words—axes, crises, diagnoses, theses; the final consonant is (z) and the preceding vowel is (i:).

When **s** is followed by (word final) silent **e** we have either (s) or (z). In the following words it is (s): base, case, decease, grease (noun), loose (adj), close (n, adj), use (n), abuse (n), excuse (n), house (n), refuse (n), diffuse (adj), premise (n, also v). In the following words it is (z): erase, close (v, also n), lose (v), grease (v), house (v), diffuse (v), refuse (v), excuse (v), abuse (v), cause (v), premise (v).

In cleanse and parse, we have (z). Otherwise, whenever 'e' is preceded by a consonant we have (s): false, pulse, sense, horses, purse. When **s** occurs in the middle of a word with vowels on both sides, we have either (s) or (z). In the following words we hear (z): artisan, partisan, courtesan, bosom, deposit, desert, disease (note the difference between disease and decease). Hesitate, miser and present. In the following words we hear (s): analysis, asylum, gasoline, generosity, courtesy, misinform, disinfect, disagree...

There is a tendency for **s** to be pronounced (z) if the following syllable is stressed. This has led to alternative pronunciation on words like disarm, dishonest, disown, and disorder.

Si, ssi, sei, ti are pronounced (sh) in compulsion, mansion, tension, version, aversion, expression, omission, passion, conscience, essential, partial, Russia. We hear a (ʒh) sound in evasion, occasion; also in pleasure, leisure, seizure, enclosure, composure, exposure, usual, visual.

We have already discussed the pronunciation of (t), (d) and (id) on the basis of the preceding consonant or vowel, in the context of the past tense marker. T is pronounced (t) in most cases. But **tu** gives us (ch): capture, departure, pasture, stature, adventure, tincture, future. But in attitude, gratitude, constitute, institute we hear (tyu:). In the following words we hear (ch) or (tyu): statue, statute, virtue, ritual.

In the following words where we have **–stion** the pronunciation is (s) followed by (ch): suggestion, congestion, digestion, combustion, question, exhaustion. In conviction, permission, promotion, sensual, sexual, pressure we hear (sh). The base words from which these are derived have (t) or (s) as the word final consonant; convict, permit, promote, sense, sex, press. In collision, erasure, decision, seizure, exposure we have (ʒ) parallel to the voiced consonants of the base words: collide, divide, erase, seize, expose (z).

Though in stressed syllables [ph] is heard as in pot, pat and paste, **ph** in spelling gives us [f] in pronunciation: phantom, pheasant, sphere, epitaph, sapphire. In 'nephew' we hear the voiceless [f] and, alternatively, the voiced [v]. Both [f] and [v] are pronounced with a frictional contact between upper teeth and lower lip. In 'Stephen' we hear only [v]. In 'shepherd' we have [p].

Q always occurs in combination with 'u'. This combination has two pronunciations [kw] and [k]. [kw] is heard in the following words loquacity, banquet, quality, squirrel, conquest, liquid. Only [k] is heard in *quay* [ki:] queue, coquette, conquer, liqueur [-ky-], liquor [-k-], mosquito, bouquet [buke:], piquant, pique [pi:k]. 'piquet' [picket] is 'a card game for 2 players, played with 32 cards'.

As **ph** gives us [f] and [v], 'th' also gives us two different fricative sounds: [θ] and [ð]. These two sounds are produced by placing the front part of the tongue behind upper teeth or teeth ridge. The main point of this pronunciation is 'friction' heard as in [*f*]. We hear [ð] in the, they them, their, though, thee, thy, thine, this, that, these, those, than, then, thence, thither, though, although, thus, fathom, father, heathen, bother, smother, mouth, (verb), breathe, southern, worthy, bathe, lathe, scathe, wreathe, blithe, writhe, clothes, scythe. [θ] is heard in thief, thing, thunder, thick, thin, thorough, thank throw three thirty, through, thistle, plinth, anthem, anthology, atheist, cathedral, orthodox, both, path eighth, north, south mouth, worth, health healthy, author, authority, authorize.

Wh gives us two pronunciations: [w] and [h]. In who, whole, whore, we hear [h]. Generally in 'wh' words we hear [w]: what, why, where, when, which whale, whirl, wheat, wheel, whistle, whine, whip, whisk, white, whiz.

X is pronounced [ks] or [gz]. [ks] is heard when the stress falls on the syllable preceding 'x' and [gz] is heard when 'x' is followed by a stressed vowel or by 'h' plus a stressed vowel. [ks] is heard in axe, relax, coax, maxim, oxygen, excite, excuse, sexton. In 'exile' we hear both [ks] and [gz]. [Gz] is heard in exact, exaggerate, exalt, examine, exult, exuberant, exhaust, exhibit, exhilarate. In the following words both [ks] and [gz] are heard: auxiliary, exhume, exotic..

In words of Greek origin with initial **x** the pronunciation is [z]: xenophobia, xanthippe, xerxes. In anxious, obnoxious, luxury we hear [ksh]. 'Luxurious' however has [gz]. 'Xerox' starts with [z]. X-mas is pronounced the way 'Christmas' is pronounced. In Quixote second syllable has [-h-] in it and the final **e** is pronounced [kwikset/kiheuti].

Y has consonantal value in the beginning of the syllables: yard, yeast, young, lawyer. Some of us tend to pronounce 'east' and 'yeast' alike. 'East' starts with a vowel [i:st] and 'yeast' starts with a consonant [yi:st]. The phonetic symbol used in dictionaries for [y] is [j].

By using vowels and consonants accompanied by stress patterns we produce words and sentences in English. Well connected sentences give us what is called 'discourse'. Discourse is spoken or written communication. It is a set of utterances (or sentences) which constitute any recognisable event of communication, e.g., a conversation, a joke, a sermon, an interview, an essay, a letter, a story, etc., Obviously this is a technical use of the term. A given discourse to be effective has to be appropriate in terms of the following criteria: (i) the main idea should be **appropriate** to the occasion; (ii) the **supporting ideas** should be appropriate to the main idea; (iii) the **format** chosen should be appropriate to the effect desired, e.g., a letter, a pamphlet, an essay, a report; (iv) the choice of **literary devices** like figures of speech, e.g., simile, metaphor) should be appropriate; (v) the choice of **words and grammatical categories** should be accurate and appropriate. What language does for us is important.

(i) We express our **experience** through language. For example, we have seen a cat chasing a mouse. The experience has three elements: a cat, a mouse and the process of chasing. The **temporal** setting is one of **before now** and the description is one of **in progress.** The sentence that we will use will be 'A cat was chasing a mouse'.

(ii) We express **logical relations** through language, e.g., I was busy writing my assignment. There was a noise. I looked in that direction. A cat was chasing a mouse. That's how I got distracted from my work'. The cause for distraction is the sound made by 'the cat's chasing of the mouse'. This cause-effect relationship is a **logical relationship.**

(iii) Language helps us strike a relationship with fellow human beings. This **interpersonal** function will be of different types. When we greet people we establish a rapport with them. This is called phatic communion. The language used for phatic communion can also be called **pleasing language.** We also use language to seek information or confirmation (questions), to make statements, to express surprise, to make requests, to give commands, etc. This kind of language can be called **telling language.**

(iv) We also express **attitudes** by making appropriate choices of words and grammatical categories. You can never make a clear-cut distinction between a fat girl and a chubby girl in terms of her appearance. Most of the time it reflects our attitude to the person or her parents. Gentleman, bloke, guy, fellow, man all may refer to 'a male human being' but the words reflect different attitudes of the speakers. Think of two salesmen reporting to their boss saying that a given job was done. One says: 'Sir, I have finished the job.' The other says: 'Sir, the job is finished.' The choice of active and passive constructions sometimes reflects mainly a difference of attitude, but not so much of experiential reality.

(v) Language expresses our choice of **topic** or **theme.** In a given situation we may like to talk about an actor, a goal or a process. For example, we can say 'a cat chased a rat', 'a rat was chased by a cat', 'the cat's chase of a rat' (provides chilling entertainment). Sometimes we can choose an adverbial as our topic: 'Yesterday, there was a light and sound show on Akbar the Great. Today, they will have a performance of Kathak.'

(vi) Language also reflects our choice of **focus.** Think of a situation where Mohan bought Sita a watch. In this sentence the normal **focus** is on watch, though with the help of **stress** we can bring any of the other elements under focus. Without using a marked stress we can change the point of focus. In 'Mohan bought a watch for Sita', Sita as a beneficiary gets emphasis. Mohan is the topic. If we want Mohan to be the topic as well as the point of focus we can say 'it was Mohan who bought a watch for Sita'. Similarly, 'it was a watch that Mohan bought for Sita' gives us **watch** under **reinforced** focus, where we are talking about watch and also focusing on it.'

Besides looking at a sentence from these angles we need to see how sentences are **forged** into a larger unit of discourse. When two sentences are part of a larger unit they will have to

cohere—both in terms of meaning and in terms of expression. Take the following sentence.

Mohan Reddy is a rich farmer from Nellore.
Mohan Reddy is a generous person.

These two sentences, as they stand are not part of a larger unit because the expression structure doesn't show their relationship. On the other hand, look at the following:

Mohan Reddy is a rich farmer from Nellore.
He is a generous person.

The use of **he** in the second sentence takes us back to the first sentence and thus **unity** is forged. Here actually his richness and his generosity are also related. On the other hand, sometimes we can face an absurd situation where an expression shows unity but meaning does not.

Mohan Reddy is a rich man.
So he is a fool.

Both **so** and **he** are forging unity but the link between richness and foolishness is not acceptable. So when we speak or write we should achieve proper unity. This is in fact a part of the logical relationship we have already talked about. Appropriate and accurate choice of words and phrases sometimes is a little tricky.

In South Indian restaurants we hear the expressions **strong coffee** and **light coffee**, quite often. A native speaker doesn't easily understand **light** and more interestingly understands **strong** differently. His antonym for **strong** is **weak**, but not **light. Strong coffee** is dark in color and has a distinct flavour, because it is made using a lot of coffee (powder). **Weak coffee** is made using a lot of water and therefore does not have a strong taste. **Black coffee** has no milk or cream in it. When you add milk or cream the drink becomes **white coffee. Light coffee**, mainly an Indian expression, refers to the quantity of milk in the drink. Milk is more or less an essential ingredient in an Indian's coffee. So when we say **strong** or **light coffee** we are referring to the quantity of milk we put in it. Might be it is the colour that has given us the expression **light coffee.** Before we add milk to it we call it decoction or regionalized variant of it as for example **dikaashanu** in Telugu. **Decoction** is 'a liquid obtained by boiling something for a long time in water'. This is not part of an average Englishman's vocabulary. So it should not be surprising if it is missed out in some dictionaries. Incidentally for us **coffee decoction** is what we get when we add coffee powder to boiled water. We don't boil coffee powder for any significant period of time. If we do, its taste will be marred.

Verbs like look, see, listen and hear also deserve special attention.

Look and **see, listen** and **hear** are parallel pairs of terms which need clear distinction.

He **looked at** her carefully and

He saw her suddenly

are acceptable sentences, but not

He saw her carefully and

He looked at her suddenly.

Similarly we can say

I tried to look at his face but in that darkness,

I couldn't see him properly.

See is 'to become aware or recognise, using one's eyes; to perceive using one's eyes'; **look** is 'to direct sight with attention'. But there are cases where the native speakers of English use **look, see** and **watch** interchangeably. Did you watch television last night? Did you see television last night? Did you look at television last night? The subtle difference we can perceive when we examine these sentences may be ignored by the hearer in a real speech situation. **Look at** may sometimes refer to the set or the reception of the set. The reply would be:

I did not watch/look at it at all (not see it).

I **watched/looked** at it for a time and then went to bed (not saw it).

I never see/watch/look at television at all these days.

A simple distinction can be kept in mind: 'See' is perceive (causally); **look at** is observe closely, (for a longer space of time); 'watch' is observe closely, usually for a longer space of time (often as part of an audience). When we see someone playing cricket, we just notice him doing what he is doing. On the other hand, when we watch him playing cricket, we observe what he is doing, when we look at him playing cricket, we are actually observing him in his game, but not his game.

One of the areas we have to acquire full understanding of the vocabulary is 'milk products'. **Cheese** is a food made from coagulated milk, separated from the **whey**, and pressed into a solid mass. **Green cheese** is 'cheese not yet dried'. **Cheddar** is 'a type of hard cheese', deriving its name from Cheddar in Somerset (England) where this type of cheese was first made. **Cottage cheese** is 'a soft white cheese made out of sour milk'. This is close to what we call **paneer**.

When two people or things are completely different from each other we say they are as different as **chalk and cheese**. Both these things may look white but they have nothing in common.

We have to be clear about the use of 'curd' and 'yogurt'. **Curd** is the coagulated substance formed from milk (often in plural). That's how Oxford English Dictionary (VoI V, 1989) defines **curd**. The New Lexicon Webster's Dictionary of the English Language (1987) defines **curd** (esp. plural) as 'the smoother thickened part of sour milk, sometimes used to make cheese'. The Random House Dictionary of the English Language (1983) says: curd (often curds), a substance obtained from milk by a coagulation, and used as food or made into cheese. Chambers English Dictionary (CED) (Allied Publishers, 1989) defines curd as 'milk thickened or coagulated by acid: the cheese part of milk, as distinguished from the whey'. Collins Cobuild English Language Dictionary (CCELD) says: 'Curds are the thick white substance which is formed when milk turns sour. It is used for making cheese'.

Whey is the watery liquid that is separated from the curds in sour milk, for example, while making cheese, if curd is used to make cheese, it cannot be the same thing as **dahi** (Hindi) or **perugu** (Telugu) or **tayr** (Tamil). As far as the native speaker is concerned curd is curdled milk. The use of plural 'curds' is justifiable because the curdled milk has in it solid pieces of curd and whey.

Yogurt (yoghurt, yoghourt), is slightly sour, thick liquid which is made from milk that has had bacteria added to it (CCELD). CED defines **yogurt** as a semi-liquid food made from fermented milk. Indian *dahi (perugu/tayr)* is ideally solid, fermented but not always sour. At present we use curd (curds) to describe our milk product. To reflect our use of the word we have to redefine, it as follows: curd (n) (also curds): a milk product, coagulated, and fermented by adding a wee bit of curd or buttermilk to milk while it is warm and then kept in a warm place. Here warmth and curd are helping the milk coagulate and ferment.

Buttermilk is the liquid that remains after the butter has been separated from the cream or curds, by churning. **Cream** is defined as a thick, fatty, yellowish-white liquid that is taken from milk and is used in cooking or poured on fruit or puddings (CCELD).

Let us now see what some bilingual dictionaries have said about **perugu** (Telugu) and **curd.** William Brown's Telugu-English Nighantuvu (Sanskrit Prachurana 44, 1953, first published 1818) describes **perugu** as the name given to sour-milk which is a favourite dish of the Indians, better known to Europeans by the name curd.

Dictionary Telugu-English by Charles Philip Brown (2nd revised edition, 1905, revised and brought up-to-date by M Venkataratnam, WH Cambell and Rao Bahadur K Veeresalingam, reissued in 1980 by the Asian Educational Services, New Delhi) defines perugu as 'curd—thick curdled milk'.

'A Dictionary—English and Telugu' by Charles Philip Brown (1853), reissued by Andhra Pradesh Sahitya Akademi (1974) gives **curd** as equivalent of **perugu. Buttermilk** is the word for **majjiga** in Telugu **chhach** in Hindi **mor** in Tamil. Brown doesn't have an entry for **yogurt,** a word of Turkish origin which obviously was not yet a popular expression. This expression is now given as an equivalent for **perugu** in A Telugu-English Dictionary by JPL Gwynn assisted by J Venkateshwara Sastry (Oxford University Press 1991).

While in this area it might be good to ramble about also neologisms.

Neologism is the term used for new words or familiar words with new meanings. We find it difficult to grasp the meaning of new words in English in spite of our English medium education whereas we find it easy to understand new words in our mother tongue. There is a basic difference between one's mother tongue and a second language or foreign language. We socialize or mature along with the acquisition of our mother tongue. In other words, our mother tongue is the language of our 'being'. The 'newness' of certain words gets easily interpreted because of the 'feel' we have for the language. Though we are surrounded by the users of English in India the quantum and quality of its use are not very conducive to a creative grasp or creative use. There are no doubt a good number of people whose own language learning faculty is so sharp and the quantum and quality of exposure to English pretty significant they more or less end up developing a native like 'feel' for English. An average Indian, however, has to be satisfied with a wee bit more than a working knowledge of English. This kind of knowledge can be compared to what a British sociologist, Professor Basil Bernstein called 'restricted code'. On the other hand a creative command of a language gives us 'elaborated code'. Some linguists say the kind of command an average Indian has of English is that of a 'semi-lingual'. A semi-lingual is one who cannot experiment and recreate his world on his own terms in the given language. The only way to grow into a full user of a language is to read the creative literature of the language and also make efforts to use it creatively. When it comes to our mother tongues like Telugu or Urdu, we have excellent exposure to it, by way of social interaction, films and magazines. More importantly we are at home with the cultural backdrop of our language whereas to some extent this is denied to us when we learn English. In other words English is more a language of 'doing' than of 'being'. Hence the inability to creatively interpret new expressions.

Here we discuss the difference that could be made between an error and an acceptable innovation. The innovation may sometimes gain currency also in the native varieties of English. Here we take up the use of 'prepone' very commonly used by Indians. This I discussed in 1993 in my column 'Mind your language' published in Deccan chronicle (Sunday edition). We have expressions like **pre-war** and **post-war, pre-independence** and **post-independence.** All these are acceptable expressions for the native speaker. When he hears **prepone** as the opposite term for **postpone** he somehow gets puzzled. His word for **prepone** is **advance.** Look at these expressions very carefully. We generally **advance** the time or day of an event whereas we **postpone** an event. In our use of English we **prepone** an event. **Prepone** is then the exact antonym of postpone. Look at the structure of **postpone.** It is made up of two Latin expressions: **post** and **ponere** (put), **postpone** then is putting something later. **Prepone** will be 'putting something before'. Structurally **prepone** is a perfect English expression. The meaning of the expression is an exact opposite of the meaning of **postpone,** whereas **advance** is not an exact antonym of **postpone**. The Concise Oxford Dictionary (Ninth Edition) has recorded **prepone** as one of its entries.

Sometimes we find ourselves inadequate in the use of ordinary words such as parts of a day. **Day** is comparable to 'din' (Hindustani). It refers to the whole day (24 hours, from midnight to midnight). It also refers to that part of the day which has light and not night (ra:t). **Day** is used also to refer to a particular period of history: the **present-day** teachers are not happy with the attitude of their students. When we **call it a day,** we decide 'to stop doing something and leave it to be finished later'. In

> he works **day in day out** preparing food for the unending stream of visitors,

'day in day out' means every day. **Daybreak** is the time in the morning when light first appears. **Dawn** is the time of the day when light first appears, just before sunrise. **Daybreak** obviously is referring to the breaking of night by the first light of the day. **Dawn** actually is referring to the descending of the light. If an idea **dawns** on us, we 'realise' it.

Morning is the first part of the day, until noon, or the time of lunch. That's why **good-morning** is the greeting used at meeting till lunch time. Later it becomes **good afternoon. Afternoon** is the time between **noon** and **evening. Noon** is **mid-day.** Originally **noon** was the ninth hour of the day in Roman and ecclesiastical reckoning—3 pm (Latin nona, the ninth). Later when the Church service called Nones was shifted to midday, the reference shifted to midday.

Morning starts immediately after midnight. That's why **the small hours** or **the wee hours** (of morning) and **early morning** refer to the period after midnight and before sunrise. **Morning sickness** is a feeling of sickness that women have in the first few months of pregnancy. **Afternoon** is the time between noon or lunchtime and 6 o' clock or **dusk** whichever is earlier. **Dusk** is the time 'just before night when the daylight has almost gone but when it is not completely dark'.

Evening is 'the time between the end of afternoon (5 or 6 pm) and the time when we go to bed'. When we meet a friend towards nightfall or later we say **Good-evening.** When friends part, then they say **good night** to each other. Interestingly we may say **good night** to a friend at 7 pm and later on say **good evening** to another friend at a meeting. **Good day** once used as a common meeting and parting greeting but it is nowadays considered a very formal expression. **Night** refers to that part of the day when it is dark outside. It is also used to refer to the period between 'the end of the afternoon and midnight'. **Nightfall** is the time when it starts to get dark. Notice the usage—**nightfall, daybreak.**

A **nightshirt** is a long, loose shirt that men and boys wear in bed whereas a **nightdress** is a sort of dress that women or girls wear in bed. Sometimes 'pyjamas' is used for 'sleeping-suit'.

Twilight is the dim light we see just after sunset or just before dawn. **Twilight** is also used to mean 'the period of decay following a period of success, vigour, greatness, etc'. **Twilight zone** is 'the decaying area of a city typically situated between the main business and commercial area and the suburbs'. **Suburbs** are the outskirts of a town or city. We can say 'subrurals' for dwellings outside the village.

Season is 'a period of the year marked by its own **typical weather conditions**'. **Spring, Summer, Autumn and Winter** are well recognized seasons. **Autumn** is the season when the weather becomes cooler and trees shed their leaves. **Deciduous** tress shed all their leaves during autumn. In horse racing **autumn leaf** is a jockey, apprentice, etc. who has often fallen from his mount. In **winter** the weather is colder than during other seasons and many of those leaf-shedding trees are now totally bare. **Spring** is the season when the weather begins to get warmer and leaves and plants start to grow again. **Summer** is the warmest part of the year.

Monsoon is the season when there is a lot of very heavy rain. Interestingly this expression is used with reference to South Asia. The British don't have any special rainy season. **Monsoon** also refers to the periodical wind of the Indian Ocean—Southwest from April to October and Northeast the rest of the year.

Rainband is a dark band in the solar spectrum due to water vapour in the earth's atmosphere. **Rainbow** is Indian

Indradhanush—'the coloured bow caused by refraction and internal reflection of light in rain drops'. A **rainbow-chaser** is a visionary, trying to achieve the impossible. A **rainy day** is a possible future time of need. **Come rain or shine** is whatever the weather or circumstances may be. **Right as rain** is perfectly in order. **To take a rain-check** is to promise to accept an invitation at a later date.

Summer pudding is made of soft fruit and bread. **Indian summer** is 'a period of warm weather during autumn'. **Summer time** is a period of time in the summer in some countries during which the clocks are put forward. This is done so that people have an extra hour of daylight in the evening.

A **wintry smile** is an unfriendly smile. **Spring onions** are the tender onions with long green leaves generally used as part of salad. A very tasty curry can be made of them. **Spring chicken** is a very young person.

A **spring roll** is a Chinese item of food consisting of a small roll of thin pastry filled with vegetables and sometimes meat and cooked in oil.

This 'season' is different from **seasoning** which we use to mean adding something to food to give relish. If **a fruit is in season** it is ripe and ready for use. If a **bitch is in season** it is on heat and ready to mate.

Similarly we sometimes get confused between 'step-' and 'half-' in the context of kinship terms. A **stepmother** is the wife of one's father other than his or her mother. A **stepbrother** is one's step parent's son by another marriage. On the other hand a **half-brother** is the son of one's mother or father by another marriage. In other words only one parent is common to them. **Stepbrothers** and **stepsisters** do not share either parent whereas **half-brothers** and **half-sisters** do.

When we look at the way people write their names we find some significant differences. Maharashtrians have a three unit name, when used in full form. The first unit is the **given**

name, the second or middle unit is the **father's name** and the third or last unit is the **family name** or **common name**—the name common to all the members of a family, for example, Yashwantrao-Balwantrao-Chauhan. Dominant Tamil pattern has two unit structure: **father's name—given name,** for example Krishnamachari-Srikkanth. Some of them add a **village name** in the beginning and a **caste indicator** like Iyer, Nadar, Pillai, Iyengar or Chettiar at the end. Here the caste name can function as a name common to all the members—at least male members—of the family and caste. The general pattern of Telugu names is: **Family name—given name.** Some people also have a general suffix like Rao or caste-specifying suffix like Naidu, Chowdhari or Reddy at the end of the name. A Sikh Punjabi name has the following pattern: **given name—Singh** for men, **Kaur** for women and a **common name.** The common name may be a caste name or sub-caste name or the name of the village, for example Bishen-Singh-Bedi. Many Punjabis in general and Sikhs in particular have sometimes shed their caste names and taken the village names as their last name.

The English-speaking world gives us a different structure of names: **First name - Middle name - Surname. First name** is the given name. **Middle name** is also given name but not generally used to call someone. The **last name** is the **surname** common to the whole clan. For example in Michael - Alexander - Kirkwood - Halliday, the name of a famous linguist, Alexander and Kirkwood are middle names given to him by his parents but never used to call him. His friends call him Michael and other scholars and students call him (Professor) Halliday.

Let's take up an important aspect of English which demands care when we use the language as the language of our secondary being.

While using any language we express one way or the other the relationship between the time of our use and the time of the event we are describing. Here we are going to reramble a few things. In terms of conceptualization we may talk of **present,**

past and **future.** But where is the 'present'? It cannot be captured because time never stops for us to look at it. However we talk of **present tense. Tense** is the dissection of **time** made (in a particular language) with reference to an event and the utterance about the event. If in 2019 we talk of an event that occurred in 2009 we will use **past tense.** On the other hand, if we want to refer to what is likely to happen later, say in 2022, we will use **future tense.** Presentness is possible only when the **time of utterance** and the **time of event** are simultaneous. When we say **I am painting** a picture, the utterance time and the event time are simultaneous. I was **painting** a picture last night shows that the time specified in 'last night' and the 'event time' (painting) are simultaneous but the event time has already 'passed off' with reference to the utterance time. When we say I will be painting a picture this weekend, the time of painting will be part of 'the weekend' to come after 'now'.

The present form 'paint' is a tense category, not a time specifier. When we say, 'she paints pictures for her living' no time is being indicated; it is the 'habit' or 'profession' that's being indicated. One thing is clear though: painting is something she started doing 'before now' and is likely to continue doing 'after now'. To that extent it is **present** subsuming both past and future time reference. This does not show that she is painting now, at the time of speaking. Actually, the **present** describes, doesn't narrate.

Tense can be properly understood if we also consider the significance of **aspect. Aspect** reflects the temporal relationship between different units of an event, whereas tense reflects the temporal relationship between utterance and event. In 'he was singing bhajans when his sister called on him', 'was singing' indicates both **past tense** and **progressive** aspect and 'called on' indicates past tense. Both 'singing' and 'calling on' are 'past' with reference to the utterance of the sentence. Singing was in progression when calling on took place. This simultaneity in past time is given in the **past progressive. Present progressive**

reflects simultaneity of an event with reference to the act of speaking—'she is singing (now)'.

In 'He has painted his car recently', we have a **present perfect** construction. **Perfective aspect** reflects completion of action and **present tense** indicates its relationship to the present state. It is important to note that we can't use a specific time adverbial with a **present perfect** verbal; we can use a non-specific time adverbial. For example, we can say, 'He has bought a house recently' but not 'He has bought a house on Monday'. This is a general rule. However, as an afterthought or as a response to a question the specific-time adverbial can be used. **Past perfect** reflects completion of action before another event, all in the 'past' with reference to the present moment of speaking. When we say, 'he had left by then' the act of 'leaving' was complete by 'then'; both 'leaving' and 'then' are 'past' relative to 'now'. 'He will have done it by the time you return' gives us future **perfect.** Both 'doing' and 'returning' will be future with reference to 'now' but 'doing' will be complete with reference to 'returning'—hence **future perfect.**

The **time adverbial** that is used with a verb is more specific, about time reference. 'My friend wrote to me today' is an interesting example. Today is present indicating the receipt of the letter from a friend who obviously wrote it a few days before today. In 'I go home tomorrow' we have 'go' with 'tomorrow', the future reference being indicated by 'tomorrow'.

The preterite forms are used to show **tense-concord.** For example, in 'she said she would buy me a pair of trousers' 'would' agrees with 'said' but doesn't reflect pastness at all. There is another interesting thing to note in this context. If you hear someone saying, 'would it be all right if I came there at 5 o' clock tomorrow?', note that both 'would' and 'came' are preterite forms but referring to future tomorrow. However 'came' is used because the action of coming will be complete at 5 o'clock and 'would' is used to agree with 'came'.

After choosing and discussing the important aspects of English it will be in order to see the problems we encounter while teaching these aspects at different levels.

For most of us in India, English is not the language of being or identities. It does not help us 'socialize' or 'mature' within our experience'. It helps us 'grow' outside our 'inner circle'.

A skill has to be identified and learnt or taught. One of the most important reasons for our children not being able to pick up adequate command of all the skills required for a good career is the 'dissociation' we see between goals and strategies. Debates and elocutions are treated as part of some programme but not as a goal-oriented activity—'good command of speech'. Letter-writing and essay-writing are practised for the purpose of passing an examination, where half of the time is spent on recollecting points for discussion. Instead, imagine a question paper where 'points' and 'relations' are given and the student has to put his writing skill to good use. When 'points' are given and their 'relations' are stated no complaint of 'out of syllabus' can be raised. The textbook, teaching and testing all will then be related exercises of identifying and developing skills.

Any teacher who is teaching a subject should develop right soft skills besides hard skills in the subject concerned. Teaching is no less of a professional career than that of an engineer or a doctor or an advocate. It is therefore appropriate that a teacher gets groomed for his profession in a full five year course, which gives him a Masters degree in Educational Technology (MEdTech). Here the content part of a chosen subject and the bases of teaching strategies and materials preparation are all blended into a solid course of subject knowledge, pedagogic and andragogic theories and practice. 'Pedagogic' when contrasted with 'andragogic' refers to teaching children whereas 'andragogic' refers to teaching adults. The difference between children and adults will be mainly felt in the choice of materials and levels of interaction. Ceteris paribus, i.e., other things being equal, children tend to learn anything well. Once they are 15 +, they prefer to learn what is interesting. Once they are 35 + they learn what is useful. Once they are 55 + they learn because they enjoy learning.

Once we recognize these differences we can design our instructions and selecting the appropriate materials will be easy. One very significant point made with regards progressive instruction is that it can be spirally organized, leading from known to unknown points.

When we teach a class, no matter what we teach, creation of meaning alone can ensure success of learning. To teach different soft skills, thinking skills and self skills, poetry, prose and drama can be fruitfully used. Poems are authentic texts, unlike constructed sentences we use while teaching grammar. Poetry is the natural spring versus distilled water. Just imagine a short poem used to teach stress patterns and pronunciation of words. Let us now see how we can use excerpts from literature for teaching different linguistic skills. Take 'As You Like It' of Shakespeare and look at this dialogue:

Rosalind : Not true in love?
Celia : Yes, when he is in, but I think he is not in.
Rosalind : You have heard him swear downright he was.
Celia : Was is not is; besides, the oath of a lover is no stronger than word of a tipster, they are both confirmers of false reckonings; attends here in the Forest on the Duke your father (Act III/SC IV).

This should be one of the most useful pieces to teach 'was', 'is', different forms of 'be' and as such the concept of tense. Rosalind's dialogue 'You have heard him swear downright he was' can be used for teaching tense concord too.

Look at these few lines from Paradise Lost:

Of man's first disobedience, and the fruit

of that forbidden tree whose mortal taste.

Brought death into the world, and all our woe
with loss **of** Eden
...
I may assert Eternal providence
And justify the ways **of** God to men
...
The mind is its own place, and in itself
Can make a Heaven **of** hell, a hell **of** Heaven.

These lines can be fruitfully used to teach different uses of 'of'. John Sinclair rightly says that **of** can be a candidate for a separate part of speech—not just another preposition. Though 'mind-heaven-hell' lines are about Satan, they can be used to teach self-skills.

Look at the following passage from Eugene O' Neill's Beyond the Horizon (Act 1, Scene 1).

"**There's** something calling me...**it's** just beauty that's calling me—the beauty **of** far off and unknown, the mystery and spell **of** the East... the freedom **of** great wide spaces, the joy **of** wandering on and on—in quest **of** the secret which is hidden over there, beyond the horizon."

This passage can be fruitfully utilized to teach 'there-' and 'it-' constructions besides the use of 'of'. This can also be used to inculcate thinking skills.

'It-' construction is best taught with lines as follows:

The man recovered of the bite.
The dog **it was** that died.
(Goldsmith's 'Elegy on the Death of a Mad Dog')

Here both 'dog' and 'died' are to be focused on, which is not possible in a simple clause like 'The dog died'. These lines show how cleft constructions are to be understood and taught.

Similarly if one wants to teach 'topical' importance as different from 'informational' importance we can look at the last stanza of Gerald Gould's Wander Thirst:

Yonder the long horizon lies and there by night and day.

The old ships draw to home again the young ships sail away.

And **come I may**, but **go I must** and men ask you why.

You may put the blame on the stars and the sun and the white road and the sky.

The third line illustrates two types of importance: importance of the topic (theme) and importance of information. The poet is talking about 'coming' and 'going' and says that the former is a matter of 'probability' (may) and the latter of 'certainly' (must). Here 'come' and 'go' are topically important and 'may' and 'must' are informationally important.

The use of 'let' in 'let's go' and 'let us go' is very interesting. In the first instance the addressee is included in 'we' whereas in the second one it is not. The following lines from Hamlet illustrate the use of 'let' in passive construction.

'Let the doors be shut upon him, that he may play the fool nowhere but in 's own house' (ACT-III/SC II: 133–4).

Hamlet also gives us an interesting use of the indefinite article:

A villain **kills** my father, and for that I, his sole son, do the same villain send to Heaven (III/II: 74–760)

This 'indefinite' article interestingly colligates with 'present' which replaces 'past'.

The evaluation system should be a natural consequence of teaching strategies. It should never test 'memory'. It should allow the students to use books, collect facts from them and then organize their discourse. It is the discourse construction that is crucial in learning a language, not facts and figures.

Let's see whether all our discussion has acceptance at our cognitive level. That is why it is often debated what ontological status one could claim for the theoretical categories and descriptive accounts of a language set up and worked out by a linguist. One is usually faced with two extreme points of view: (i) the 'psychological or mental' point of view of a 'realist' which claims that the description and the categories that go with it should in a sense unconsciously exist in a speaker's mind—a view held by different people with different degrees of vagueness; (ii) the 'descriptive convenience' point of view which is held by people with different degrees of seriousness. Between the two extremes can be placed the notion of 'perceptual plausibility'.

Grammars based on this principle of 'perceptual plausibility' can make a claim not to 'correctness' and 'mental reality' but to 'plausibility', 'appropriateness' and 'functional validity'. The last claim should be understood to mean that a grammar is a 'grammar' only when its description is valid functionally for the language, irrespective of the formal notation and methodology used by it. A grammar which is not valid for the language remains at the stage of a set of hypotheses to be verified and rewritten. The notion of 'functional validity' given here should be distinguished from that of the realists who claim that the rules of their grammar actually operate in the use of the language concerned.

If the phonological description of a language is seconded by the underlying features of a language game, we can confidently claim 'sociological reality' and thence 'perceptual plausibility' to that description. We want to justify our analysis by bringing in a language game Telugu children play. The game is called the '--ŋgv' game (v:vowel). In disyllabic or trisyllabic words, '--ŋg' is inserted between the first and second syllable and it acquires the vowel of the first syllable and the cluster feature of length follows '--ŋg V'. for example:

Actual word language game form:

V

1. Ka ru: ka:ru (black) kaŋga:ru V

C
2. Ka ru: karru (plough share) kaŋgarru C
N
3. Pa ḍu: paṇḍu (fruit) paŋgaṇḍu --N
Y
4. Ku pu: kaypu (intoxication) kaŋgaypu --Y
W
5. Ka lu: kawlu (lease) kaŋgawlu --W
W
6. Ka gili: kawgili (embrace) kaŋgawgili --W

Here length features V, C, N, –Y, –W are treated as formative (syllable-complex) features or word-features, not as segmental features.

Our 'word-feature' concept is able to explain the pattern underlying the language game under consideration. If we had adopted the usual analysis of segmentalizing the length phenomenon we will be talking about long vowels and diphthongs in the language: a:, i:, u:, e:, o:, ay, aw and treat consonantal length as repeated consonants. We cannot ignore the fact that all length features are treated alike by the game.

Here we can mention another interesting piece of evidence in favour of our claim to 'sociological reality' for our cluster-feature treatment of length phenomena in Telugu. The piece of evidence invoked here is an instance of metathesis. When he was about five years old, my son produced a metathesized form for the Telugu word when he wanted an extra helping of cooked rice.

Actual form	Metathesised form
C	C
a na mu (annamu)	a ma nu (ammanu)

Here it is pretty clear that the onset consonants of second and third syllables have exchanged their positions and the length feature remains intact. This change at the phonological level accounts for the phonetic output quite easily.

These two instances of language game and metathesis make two points:

(i) 'length' has to be abstracted as a special feature.

(ii) Changes for the language games and metatheses are made at the phonological level, not at the phonetic level.

When we transcend the threshold of monolingualism (use of one language only) we ramble into the arena of translation. We may have to keep in mind that translation can be used to help in the teaching of a nonlocal language. Similarly translation is used to create a discourse in another language. To take care of this it may be useful to look at translation both in terms of ideation and in terms of praxis.

We 'translate' our experience into a discourse, a theory into practice, ideals into action, etc. For our discussion; here we concentrate on 'interlanguage transfer of message'. This takes 'message' as constant and 'language' as variable. But any careful comparison of an 'original' text and its 'translation' will display difference in the thesis or content.

Content could be semantic (code-based) or pragmatic (coder-based). Semantic content is reflected in the lexicogrammar and phonology of a language. Pragmatic content, on the other hand, is derived from the sociocultural or situational background of the users of language. Wherever extrasentential or extralinguistic information has to be brought in to explain the content of an utterance, we are within the pragmatic orchard. But on the other hand where the lexicogrammatical items and phonological features reflect the content we are within the semantic mansion. Whatever is 'denoted' by a lexical item directly will be a bundle of sememes and whatever is 'connoted' will be a cluster of pragmemes.

Let's look the following pairs of lexical items:

1. Master X Slave
2. Senior X Junior

The lexeme 'slave' will have as one of its constituents the sememe of SUBSERVIENCE. On the other hand the lexeme 'junior' will not have it as its sememe. 'Master', 'husband', 'father' and 'friend' will yield us a cline of 'authority' to 'non-authority'. Somewhere in the middle we may even have a semantico-pragmatic threshold. It is very important to note that semantic change may consist of interchange of sememes and pragmemes.

Repetition of an expression in SL should not be ignored while structurating the expression in TL. What is 'unsaid' and 'implied' should remain so if our desire is to **transtext** the text from SL to TL. The so-called free translation of course does not do this nor does it intend to do so. Semantics of translation refers to the crux of **transmeaning**. Meaning in all its colours should be 'recreated' if one could do so. In English 'dear' has at least two meanings: 'expensive', 'loved'. Similarly in Telugu priyam (aina) has both these meanings. So a translator should choose this word which is not nonambiguous.

The pragmatics of translation refers to the purpose of translation. Literature—especially scriptural—needs 'superspecial' care in translation. If we want the text in the TL to be an authoritative text no omission is possible, nor any addition.

Here I will take a few scriptural texts and illustrate the points I have been making. Sukhmani Sahib is part of 'Sri Guru Granth Sahib', the holy book of the Sikhs. This has been rendered into English by Professor Teja Singh under the title 'The Psalm of Peace' (1963). I present here the second canto of the text:

Prabh ke simrani garabhi na base

Prabh ke simrani dukh jamu nase

Prabh ke simrani kalu parahare

Prabh ke simarni dusmanu tare

Prabh simrat kachchu bighanu na lage

Prabh ke simrani anudin jage
Prabh ke simrani bhau na biape
Prabh ke simrani dukh na santape
Prabh ke simranu sadh ke sangi
Sarab nidhan Nanak hari rangi.

Teja Singh's translation reads as follows:

If a man meditates on the name:
He will not go through the round of births
He will be immune from the torture of Death
And will shed off all mortality
His enemies will keep away from him
And he will be safe from all harm
His mind will be always on the alert
And all will not be affected by fear or troubled by pain
This meditation is learnt in the company of the holy
All riches in abundance for him who is God-intoxicated!

A comparison of the two texts given above shows that the translator has not repeated 'Prabh ke simrani' of the SL text in the TL text. This kind of choice can technically be called 'tampering'. Whenever we tamper with a given text we end up interpreting a text, not creating a parallel text, which we have called 'transtexting'.

In a scriptural text we find both **entropy** and **redundancy** in abundance. Entropy refers to the underavailability of signals 'for communication' and redundancy to 'overavailbility of signals for communication'. Repetition of an expression comes under redundancy. This is well utilized in scriptural texts to achieve what I call SMALL UNIT AUTONOMY (SUA). Believers tend to quote from scriptures and they will find it handy to do so if one-line or two-line units are self-sufficient. Repetition also helps in drilling a point well into the minds of the believers. A translator cannot ignore these factors if he wants to transtext.

Let's look at a different aspect of scriptural translation. Look at the different versions of St. Mathew 16:18:

1. Also, I say to you, you are Peter, and on this rockmass I will build my congregation, and the gates of Ha'des will not overpower it [New world Translation of the Holy Scriptures (NWT)].
2. And I say also unto thee, that thou art Peter, and upon this rock I will build my Church: and the gates of Hell shall not prevail against it [Authorised Version (AV)].

Interestingly 'hell' doesn't occur anywhere in NWT. Also see Isaiah 5:14:

1. Therefore she'ol has made its soul spacious and has opened its mouth wide beyond bounds: and what is splendid in her, also her crowd and her uproar and the exultant one will certainly go down into it (NWT).
2. Therefore hell hath enlarged herself, and opened her mouth without measure, and their glory, and their multitude, and their pomp, he that rejoiceth, shall descend into it (AV).

Gehenna, Ha 'des, She'ol, Tartarus are the words found in NWT whereas AV uses 'hell' for all these words:

MATHEW 5:22

1. …whereas whoever says, 'you despicable fool! Will be liable to the fiery Ge'hen'na (NWT)
2. ..but whosoever shall say thou fool shall be in danger of hell fire (AV)'.

PETER 2:4

1. Certainly if God did not hold back from punishing the angels that sinned, but by throwing them into Tartarus delivered them to pits of darkness reserved for judgment (NWT).

2. For if God spared not the angels that sinned, but cast them down to hell, and delivered them into chains of darkness, to be reserved unto judgement (AV).

The choice of NWT not to use 'hell' for four different words seems to be a 'theological choice' warranted by the use of different words in the original texts. On the other hand the AV seems to have gone in for just one word in English probably due to conceptual convergence. Similar is the case with the word 'love' which in the English version represents some of the following words given in the Greek for LOVE: **Storge** (familiar love), **Ludus** (playful love), **Mania** (obsessive love), **Pragma** (enduring love), **Philautia** (self love), **Philios** (brotherly love), **Eros** (love between man and women) and **Agape** (unconditional divine love).

The translation of a scriptural text if intended to be used as a scriptural text warrants the super-special care we have talked about. Similarly, a literary piece needs that care if the TL version is to be treated as a piece of literature. If the purpose is just to 'inform' or 'interpret,' one may have a little more freedom. If a writer takes an SL text as just a source of inspiration to create a new text in the TL we have a free translation. Even in the case of a scriptural text or similar texts the translator may make a sociological choice or political choice to drop certain parts or go in for tampered translation. For example if a translator of the Bhagavad Gita chooses to render VARNA as 'class', not as 'caste', he is making a choice. Similarly, if he translates Brahmana as 'Seeker of Truth' or 'Scholar' not as Brahmin he is keeping in mind the differences in the connotation of the word as used in ancient times and now.

To sum up, the pragmatics of translation decides the type of translation one has to go for. Scriptural texts need super-special care if the purpose is to transtext. Literary texts also need special care if the original is intended to be re-presented in TL. If the intention is to create a new text, only inspired by the original, we have a 'free' translation. Nonliterary texts also can offer us a choice. If the purpose is to strictly present the views of the original author in his or her name we have to be careful. If the purpose is to inform or interpret one can be relaxed in his translation.

Sometimes translations are spontaneous and humorous. When asked for the Telugu equivalent of WALNUTS, Rajitha, a graduate salesgirl of Heritage Foods, blurted out GODA GINZALU. GODA in Telugu is for WALL and GINZALU is for NUTS. This is an idiomatic expression, a nonserious translation though.

If text is the 'given' for our study, what we comprehend is actually what we perceive as discourse. 'Text' is the constant and discourse is the variable, and the discourse perceived depends on the perceiver's background and disposition. The background comprises the **talent**, the **training** and the **toil** (the three T's) of the perceiver. The disposition can be the motivated bias or personal mood of depression, enthusiasm or excitement, ideological stand and academic orientation.

Let's be clear on one point. No perception is objective; all interpretation is bound to be subjective. The rationale we come out with, the evidence we show and the language we use to present it will make it much more objective than it could be otherwise. If, for example, we develop a semiotic orientation, and also keep Claude Levi Strauss's view of mythology as our guide, then we perceive the Puranas and the Counter-Puranas of different cultures totally differently. Many of us know that for Puja only cow milk is used. This should be due to the fact that buffaloes were yet to be domesticated. In addition, this act of domestication by a farmer woman could have become the base for Mahishasuramardani legend. Mahishi is a she-buffalo. Asura, according to Valmiki, was used only to refer to Daityas, the children of Diti, because they refused to drink sura whereas Adityas, the children of Aditi, were called Suras because they accepted sura. Valmiki does not refer to Ravana as Asura. Ravana was called Rakshasa. Valmiki says Brahma the Swyambhu Adideva created Yakshas and Rakshasas to safeguard sea-routes. In the Gita, Paramatma says that he is Prahlada among Daityas and Kubera among Yaksha-Rakshsas. Later literature conflated Daityas (Asuras), Rakshasas and Danavas (the children of Danu) into one group. Similarly the legend of Manmatha being burnt by Shiva and then telling Rati that she could see him could be the beginning of dressing up. All the Pativrata stories could have been spun to stabilize the concept of family and spousal relations.

When we compare a text written in a language with a transcreated text we will certainly find some differences. The transcreated text may or may not reflect the flavour of the original language and culture. The quantum of such reflection may depend upon the intention of the translator, the purpose of the translation and authenticity of the translation. We may now look at how we create discourse in films. Technically this is not translation but in reality all texts are translations from our thinking. We now look at a text discussing different aspects of NT Rama Rao a famous Telugu film star, producer, and director of the 20th century.

Some stories are 'event-oriented' and some others are 'personality-oriented'. The former answers the question 'What?' and the latter 'Who?' It is in this context we will talk about the semiotics of character portrayal.

The following parameters are useful to discuss the characters in a film.

1. Familial
2. Social
3. Personal.

The first parameter 'locates' the character in a given family where he or she has certain paradigmatic and syntagmatic relations with other characters. The second parameter 'identifies' the character as part of a social structure where he has certain obligations and privileges. The third parameter is engendered by the first two parameters. This parameter gives the character his or her unique status. The personal parameter needs to be analysed in terms of the following sub-parameters:

PERSONAL

1. Self esteem
2. paradigmaticity
3. syntagmaticity
4. semanticity (significance)
5. pragmaticity (value)
6. rationality
7. Emotionality
8. mobility
9. physique
10. make up
11. physical movements
12. praxis—verbal/nonverbal.

These twelve sub-parameters are proposed as possibilities, not as an exhaustive list. A narrative which aims at focusing on the multidimensionality of a character 'surrenders' the plot movement to the unravelling of the character. On the other hand where the complexity of events is being focused upon, the characters are 'surrendered' to develop the plot.

A film can be viewed from three angles:

1. Diagesis
2. Genre and symbol
3. Personae

Diagesis designates 'the sum of film's denotation: the narration itself'.

Genre sets the 'tone' of the film whereas symbol decides the purpose and ethos of the film. In other words it reflects the ideology of the movie/movie maker. The 'personae' angle gives us the characters we have already started looking at in detail. All these parameters and categories are interdependent and overlapping too.

NT Rama Rao (NTR) portrayed the following characters of mythological importance: Shiva, Valmiki, Rama, Ravana, Indrajit, Bheeshma, Sri Krishna, Arjuna, Brihannala, Bheema, Kichaka, Dushyanta, Srinivaasa (Venkateswara).

Ravana as a devotee, egoist, lover of fine arts and beauty, logician and adventurer are all portrayed for us by NTR. The way Ravana lifts Mount Kailas and later opens up his entrails and plays Rudra Veena are to be seen to realize the true artistic excellence achieved by NTR the actor and the director in 'Sita Rama Kalyanam'.

The way Krishna is portrayed really baffles us. This is like Kirk Douglas playing the role of Lord Jesus. Krishna defies most attempts at definitions. His graceful smile, romantic disposition, diplomatic manoeuvres, refusal to be provoked, furious if provoked, omniscient innocence are diametrically opposed to what Ravana and Duryodhana stand for. But NTR actually has set a pattern for the Sri Krishna character.

'Sita Rama Kalyanam' is an 'epic' (genre). The purpose of the movie is to prepare the background for the later part of the Ramayana. The ethos of the movie is one of 'elevation'. Here Ravana, Rama, Surpanakha, Sita, Mandodari, Dasharatha, Vishwamitra, Lakshmana, Vibhishana, Kumbhakarna—are portrayed in terms of their 'nature' and 'nurture'.

The thesis of Sita Rama Kalyanam can be atomized on the following lines:

1. Ravana's lifting of Mount Kailash, with the Shiva Stuti on his lips.
2. Ravana opening his entrails and playing them as the Rudra Veena
3. Ravana excluding 'nara' (humans) and 'vanara' (monkeys) from the list of his targets.
4. Ravana's meeting with Lord Shiva

5. Ravana's confrontation with Nandi
6. Ravana's confrontation with Matulungi
7. Ravana searching for Vishnu
8. Ravana's soldiers harassing hermits and women
9. Lord Vishnu's promise to the devatas (angels)
10. Ravana's confrontation with Rambha and Nalakubala's curse on Ravana.
11. Ravana's confrontation with Vedavati
12. Ravana bringing Vedavati's ashes home.
13. Mandodari sending the ashes abroad
14. Rakshasas burying the ashes in Janaka's Kingdom
15. Putrakameshti Yajna
16. The birth or Rama, Bharata, Lakshmana and Shatrughna
17. Janaka getting baby girl in the furrow made by the plough used by him.
18. The princes being taught by their guru.
19. Viswamitra taking Rama and Lakshmana with him for 'Yaga Rakshana' (protection of yajna).
20. Viswamitra teaching the two brothers 'bala' and 'atibala' vidyas
21. The episode of Ahalya
22. Rama killing Tāṭaka
23. Sita and Mandodari praying to Durgamata
24. Ravana's failure to lift Shiv Dhanush
25. Rama breaking the Dhanush
26. Ravana's meeting with Parashurama
27. Rama draws up the power of Parashurama
28. Rama's marriage with Sita.

In almost all these episodes the verbal praxis is as important as the nonverbal praxis. The emphasis is on character and the 'elevation' of all the important personae.

As part of the diagesis one has to mention also the following, besides the main episodes mentioned above.

1. Ravana's travel in Pushpak.
2. Rama and Lakshmana preparing a protective shield of arrows over the Yajnashala.
3. Avataara Varnana, the narration of Lord Vishnu's incarnations, in dance form, heralding the birth of Rama and others.
4. Mandodari and Ravana entertaining each other—the former singing and the latter playing on his veena.
5. Lord Shiva and Parvati dancing on Mount Kailas.
6. The ten heads of Ravana disappearing one after the other when Shiva presses his foot on the Mount.
7. The sound of the birds in the forest.

The scene where Ravana lifts the mountain on his ten heads shows rivers flowing on the mountain. The use of the 'Shiva stuti' (hymn to Shiva), a composition of Ravana himself, in the scene has telling effect on the audience.

Now back to my academic life at York. Dr Chekuri Ramarao of Osmania wrote to me asking me to go to London to meet Professor Bh Krishnamurthy at Indian YMCA building and also give him a small amount of British currency. When he reached the USA, Professor Krishnamurthy sent me a copy of the Sound Pattern of English by Noam Chomsky and Morris Halle, a great theoretical work with lot of discussion of English phonology. The ideas presented in Part 4 of the book will be of great value to any phonologist trained to understand the basics of speech organization. I am very happy to mention that Chomsky gave me a good four page reply to a letter of mine raising the concept of markedness and the way they handled it and the way M. MAK Halliday and Paul Postal handled it.

I had worked on a comparative study of English and Telugu Syntax for my Postgraduate Research Diploma thesis (1968).

The revised version of it was published as monograph 5 of CIE (1970). Now I wanted to work on phonology, and the background reading of it I had done while at CIE. It was a wonderful accident that JR Firth, the great British linguist was from Yorkshire. His student was MAK Halliday also from Yorkshire and his student was my teacher Dr SK Verma who supervised my work on syntax. Now my supervisor was Dr MW De Silva, a Sri Lankan, who did his MA by thesis under the supervision of JR Firth at School of Oriental and African Studies. Here Firth was my grandguru but in my syntax he was my great-grand guru.

The title of my thesis at York was 'A Systemic Treatment of Certain Aspects of Telugu Phonology'. Telugu is a Dravidian Language. Though a Dravidian language, Telugu has absorbed from Sanskrit a good number of lexical items and also phonological features like aspiration. Modern Spoken Telugu uses a good number of English words like guarantee, road, bus, car, school, doctor, bucket, ticket, train, donation and promotion. Being, as it was, the National Foreign Language, English has made serious inroads into Telugu, contributing lexical items and also phonological features like friction as in 'f' of coffee.

We will start with an interesting phenomenon that differentiates Telugu from English. Agreement between Subject and verb is realised as **Gender-Number-Person** (GNP) reflector. Since the reflection is of the subject we can call it Subject Reflex (SR). In some languages it is object that is reflected and in some it may be both Subject and Object. In Telugu gender is reflected in the verb only when the Subject is the third person singular pronoun or a singular noun.

Let's now have a brief preview of Telugu clauses. We take three types of clauses for the preview. First we will take a verbless clause reflecting relationship between two nominals.

1.	a. nenu ame anna<u>nu</u>.	b. nuvvu evari<u>vi</u>?
	I her elder brother SR.	You who SR?
	"I (am) her elder brother."	"Who (are) you?"

Here the Complement reflects the subject. This SR phenomenon is absent in the complement when the Subject is in the third person singular, pronoun or noun:

c. ratan ame anna.
Ratan her elder brother.
"He (is) her elder brother."

2. a. palu levu.
Milk aren't SR.
"Milk isn't available."

b. palu unnāyā?
milk are Qn?
"Is there some milk?"

In (2) we have an existential clause. In Telugu palu (milk) is always in the plural with an extremely rarely used pāyi as its singular counterpart.

3. a. Maa anna ninna karu konnāḍu.
Our elder brother yesterday car bought SR.
"My brother bought a car yesterday."

b. āme anna ninna emi konnadu?
Her elder brother yesterday what bought.
"What did her brother buy yesterday?"

In (3a) and (3b) we have actional clauses.

In the three clauses (1, 2, 3) we have seen above there is a subject-Reflex which gives 'finiteness' to the verbal group or complement and thence to the clause. If the clauses are prosodically marked for fall or rise tone, the finiteness is reinforced by the free tone group tone. If the tone is 'rise-fall' or 'fall-rise' the tone group will have the 'expectant tone group' status. The grammatical 'finiteness' and phonological 'freedom' are complementary, the latter having superimposing value in complex cases.

Now about my life in York. TV was new to me and I was watching cricket on TV while in the university and watched news and entertainment programme while at home. On an average, I spent physically with books about two hours a day, while brooding on what I read at Hyderabad and at York went on unimpeded except while in sleep. We don't really know what rains in the brain and what brain reins in while in sleep.

Five months before I submitted my thesis I went to my supervisor and said that I would write five chapters. He responded saying: "Now you are on the right track." I had told him one year before that I would write 15 chapters, which obviously he did not think plausible but did not say so. I asked him why he did not show his disapproval when I had planned fifteen chapters earlier. He gave a reply which is useful for every supervisor: "This is your thesis. If you think about it you grow. If I think about it I grow." This I kept in mind while supervising my students. I encouraged them to develop their own theoretical work and I never dictated anything or wrote anything for them. Every student is a potential international scholar. We have to encourage them to grow on their own and also help them be firm in their resolve to excel.

British universities treat their research scholars as very important inputs for their excellence. Whenever a scholar asked for a copy of a research paper they would get it from some other library if they did not have it in theirs.

I don't mind being a little immodest here. To exempt me from the first year BPhil course I was given a take-home test of a set of data and was to write a grammar of it. And I did it pretty easily because I was already trained by Dr Verma in the handling of data and using theoretical concepts to describe a text. Besides, I had already used Koutsudas's 'Writing Transformtional Grammars', while doing my PGRDTE. When the examiner went through the answers, he was surprised: "After four years of training in linguistics our students don't handle it deftly. How could you do it?" Then I told him about Dr Verma and his guidance and the way he made me read several thousand pages of linguistic analysis. I will not be totally modest when I refer to an incident of 1997 at Cardiff and the occasion was International Systemic Functional Congress. After I gave a

15 minutes talk on Firthian Prosodic Analysis and the way I developed Systemic Phonology on its base, an Australian linguist came to me and said: "I envy you. You know so much about Firth." I replied that the whole credit goes to Dr Verma who made me read everything written by Firth, Firthians, Halliday and Hallidayans. This I would say also speaks well of the wonderful library of Central Institute of English (later Central institute of English and Foreign Languages and now the English and Foreign Languages University). It will be appropriate to mention the help given those days by The British Council and the Ford Foundation in the strengthening of the Institute and the library. Especially in those early years when Prof VK Gokak and Prof Ramesh Mohan during its formative years and later Prof SK Verma during its strengthening decades deserve all credit. The librarians who really developed the library deserve to be mentioned, first Mr Risvadkar and later Mr LS Ramaiah during its growing years and strengthening years.

During my stay at York as a research scholar I was also asked to conduct seminars for the BA (Hons) students. Two people whose names I remember are Geoffrey K Pullam who became a famous linguist and theoretician. Along with others he developed Generalised Phrase Structure Grammar. The other one is Professor Goyaverts, another great scholar from Belgium. Geofrey Pullam was of great help to me in editing my thesis for submission (1972).

In the month of January 1972 I went to my supervisor and submitted three chapters. He okayed them and asked me to submit my thesis within a fortnight, with the understanding that the viva would be held after a month. I pleaded for more time because I was yet to submit the next two chapters. He responded saying there was no need to see the next two chapters and I could include them and submit the thesis. He added that I should present a spectrographic analysis of a few sentences to illiustrate the generalizations I made about intonation. After

I submmited my thesis he said that I had deviated a lot from Firth and so he was appointing an extra examiner and he was withdrawing from the examinership. He also advised me to send a copy of it to MAK Halliday. After a week he announced the date of viva voce and also said Prof Asher (Edinburgh) and Prof EJA Henderson (SOAS London) would come for the viva. The day arrived. The examiners congratulated me for doing so much of work in a period of two years.

Success no doubt depends on so many factors. My wife was a monumental support in not only verifying the authenticity of data and also making my life one of love and happiness. The correct guidance and support by the supervisor was of great value. The monetary support of the university and the administrative support of the department of language were of immense value.

York is the second oldest city of England, the first being London. The Mayor of York is called Lord Mayor just like the Lord Mayor of London. We also have Archbishop of York just like, but not equal to, the Archbishop of Canterbury, the chief of the Church of England. It may be mentioned in passing that the Monarch of England and the Prime Minister of England cannot be Catholics. Except for such traditional restrictions the United Kingdom (Northern Ireland, Great Britain (including England, Wales, and Scotland) is a secular country.

York is famous for York Minster. When I was there I visited the Minster and saw how the huge construction was raised up totally with the help of cranes for them to repair the foundation. This was quite a technological feat reflecting both the commitment and competence of the people. Much later somewhere in the late in 80s I mentioned it to a film journalist and a Muslim from South India. This was at Punjabi University Patiala, before the demolition of the Babri Masjid. I said a similar thing could be done with the Babri Masjid. It can be lifted and put on a nearby location leaving the site for the Ram temple. Similar arrangement could be made for the Varanasi and Mathura temples. That rationalist journalist replied: "Dr Prakasam you are right. One can strike a compromise and do something with a couple of places. But don't forget some people have a list of 200 masjids built on demolished temples. Any serious attempt will undermine our status and we will become second-grade citizens, which no one likes." We should not jump to any negative conclusion treating this as a political statement. A similar incident took place at the Punjabi University Patiala where I spent eleven and half years in the department of Anthropological Linguistics. The Sikhs of the campus got a piece of land to build a Gurudwara on the campus. The Hindus also expressed the desire to have a temple and asked the Vice Chancellor for a piece of land. I went to the chairman of the committee asking for a piece of land for the temple and said we could develop a temple around the Shivaling which was already there in the nursery. His reply reminded me of what my journalist friend said: "Dr Prakasam the problem is not a temple. At present we are equal to the Sikhs and if we don't get a piece of land we could be treated as second to them." Isn't there a method in the common response of community to a given situation? Ultimately we were given a piece of land on which a Laxmi Narayana Mandir was built. This incident is important to note that any hasty conclusion is inimical to comperhensive thinking.

While in England I visited Leeds University to attend a seminar and visited Bradford to buy Indian groceries. Patak Spices, an Indian condiment shop run by an Indian who had migrated from East Africa, used to supply Indian groceries including basmati rice from East Pakistan (now Bangladesh) and other items like papad and betel leaves. The Railways would bring parcels and deliver at home. Then we would send the money to London.

It is generally said that an Englishman's home is his castle. A policeman would need a warrant to enter the house and arrest someone. I remember an incident when a policeman came to our house and met my landlord Mr Aditiba. The policeman wanted him to come out of the house because he could not enter the house. My smart landlord refused to go out. The door was opened but he was inside the house and the policeman outside the house. Later the landlord told me that the policeman had come to take him to the police station because he had not paid some fine. The policeman did not enter his house and always addressed him as 'sir'.

Here I would like to mention what my children did with his name. His name was Aditiba and they used to call him Pitati. Now let us examine how Aditiba became Pitati:

$a_1 \quad d_2 \quad i_3 \quad t_4 \quad i_5 \quad b_6 \quad a_7$

$p_6 \quad i_3 \quad t_2 \quad a_1 \quad t_4 \quad i_5$

If one observes carefully, the children's version has all the sounds of the adult version but with two changes: 'd' and 'b' became 't' and 'p' which means voiced sounds became voiceless and the arrangement of consonants and vowels was changed. The final syllable 'pa' was placed in the beginning. The medial syllable comes later and a syllable is dropped.

In 1972 before coming to Hyderabad I had applied for a lectureship in linguistics at the CIE. I was considered in absentia and taken. I came back to India in March and joined the Institute as a lecturer. In no time I was persuaded to apply for a lectureship in the Department of Linguistics of the Osmania University. On September 9, 1972, I joined the Osmania University and stayed there till December 1978. From June 1977 to December 1978 I was on deputation to the Union Public Service Commission as Under Secretary.

While at Osmania I widened my knowledge of linguistics with continuous discussion with colleagues, seminars, presentations and teaching of different subjects. Dr B Lakshmibai gave me a copy of Hockett's A Course in Modern Linguistics and asked me to read it, saying, 'not having read Hockett' was my weakness. Dr Chekuri Ramarao had already guided me in the area of traditional Telugu grammar. Before I went to UK for my PhD, both of us used to live in Vidyanagar, just a couple of kilometres away from the Osmania University and the CIE.

The Advanced Centre of Linguistics at Annamalai University used to conduct seminars regularly on different languages. I presented many papers in English but mainly on Telugu. Similarly Professor VI Subramoniam from Kerala University, department of linguistics, appreciated my work and encouraged me. He invited me to a seminar and later made me one of the three secretaries of Dravidian Linguistics Association (DLA) started by him. Professor VI Subramoniam started the International journal of Dravidian Linguistics as a publication of the DLA.

In 1972 December we had the second All India Conference of Indian Linguistics Association. I was not well, I had to dictate a paper and by chance Prof Kumaraswamyraja of Annamali University appreciated my paper and mentioned it to Prof Ashok Kelkar. That was my first meeting with him when he called me and sat with me for half an hour going through my paper and giving suggestions for improvement. He also advised me to send it to the Indian Linguistics for publication after revision. This particular paper Morpheme Revisited looks at the concept of minimal grammatical unit differently from what was usually taught in the classroom and was very close to the Bloomfieldian ideas. The Post-Bloomfieldian theory can be called static morphology whereas the Bloomfieldian model is process morphology.

Different forms a morpheme takes in different contexts are treated as equivalents in static morphology whereas in process morphology one alternative taken as the basic one and the other as derived. For example 'S' (cats), 'Z' (dogs), 'IZ' (horses) are three variants available to reflect plurality. We can take -Z as the basic alternant and derive -S and -iz as variants to suite the final consonant of the base word. On the other hand in static morphology all the three variants are taken as of equal status.

This leads us to believe 'Z' occurs after voiced consonants and vowels which are voiced anyway. This is not convincing. There are many words in English which have 's, p, t' after vowels. On the other hand we can say -s occurs after voiceless consonants, -iz occurs after sibilants (S,Z) and affricates (*ch*as in *ch*in, 'J' as in villa*ge*) and 'Z' elsewhere which always includes post-vowel and post nasal position.

Besides being a lecturer in linguistics at Osmania University Arts College, I was also given the responsibility of being the Mess Warden of the Old PG hostel. Now it's called the Manjeera Hostel. The main warden was Dr N Yadagiri Reddy of the Psychology Department. Both of us were chosen by Dr Narayankaran Reddy of the Department of Philosophy and who was at that time the Vice-Principal of the college.

Justice P Jaganmohan Reddy who joined as Vice Chancellor completely changed the negative impression the university had among the public, with a lot of hard work and determination. As long as he was there he did his best to see that copying was not allowed and unauthorised occupancy in hostel was eliminated. Unfortunately centralization of exams was opposed by some students because copying would not be allowed. Some students went on a hunger strike against the centralization and some of the students from Old PG hostel. Dr Yadagiri Reddy and I paved the way for the compromise: the students will get special handouts and fifteen days of intensive teaching. The Vice Chancellor was happy and he invited Dr Yadagiri Reddy to takeover as Chief Warden. I encouraged him to take it. I generally follow the principle that if we say no to take up a responsibility we lose the right to evaluate a person who has taken up the responsibility. I also put it in the form of sermon: ***don't seek anything*** and ***don't flee anything.***

Most of the time I assisted Dr Yadagiri Reddy in the management of all the hostels of the University. The Vice Chancellor sanctioned special funds to refurbish the hostels by getting them vacated for the summer. Admissions were strictly on the basis of commitment to follow discipline. An inter-hostel youth festival was held which was a roaring success. As a precursor to it every hostel conducted its own competitions and celebrated it as the Hostel Day. The Vice Chancellor visited our hostel for the Hostel Day. The wards of our hostel were progressive and they did not want to spend the money on prizes for the winners. Instead they suggested that the money should be used to buy clothes for the workers. When I mentioned it at the meeting the Vice Chancellor appreciated by clapping which others followed. My response was a little terse. I said, "Mere clapping is not enough. We should do something special for the students."

Here is the photograph of Vice Chancellor's visit to our hostel along with others.

From left to right: Principal Muttalib, Vice Chancellor P Jaganmohan Reddy, Dr N Yadigiri Reddy, Dr Narayankaran Reddy, Dr Andhraiah, and me.

A couple of weeks later there was a meeting of all the wardens and senior professors with the Vice Chancellor. Unimpeded vocalization of my ideas and feelings has always been my strength and my weakness. I raised my hand in the meeting and the Vice Chancellor asked me to speak out. I suggested that every hostel should have a small library of its own so that the students can use their precious time fruitfully. One senior professor objected to it saying students just waste their time and they would not be using the library. The Vice Chancellor's response reflected magnanimity in several senses. He said: "I love that young man, the one who said mere clapping is not enough and something should be done for the students. Yes, we will have libraries in every hostel and I will sanction 10,000 rupees per hostel." This incident showed that Justice Jaganmohan Reddy was a fair-minded and generous person who knew when to be strict and when to be liberal. This is the quality of a great person. The newspapers commended the good work done for the hostels. THE INDIAN EXPRESS in its issue of March 20, 1976 made a special mention of it and said:

> "Osmania University campus hostels have undergone a sea change in the last ten months... Dr N Yadigiri Reddy, Chief Warden and Dr V Prakasam, Additional Warden, PG hostel were chiefly responsible for this change."

I remember an incident which will be useful to others. I once visited Dr Narayanakaran Reddy's home. I was a little foolishly discontented because there was no immediate possibility of becoming a reader. I don't remember exactly what he said but he was successful blowing off the cobweb off discontentment. I think that effected a permanent cure. I don't remember to have felt bad about any situation later.

Professor Kostic of Yugoslavia had collaboration with the department regarding speech pathology and speech rehabilitation. As part of that collaboration there was a two day seminar on phonetics. I was given a topic for presentation: laryngeal features. This is a pure phonetic topic and I had to work on it very hard. The books of Malmberg, De Lattre, Abercrombie had much to offer by way of ideas and dis cussion. The paper turned out to be rich and it was deeply appreciated by others. Only a couple of colleagues were unhappy that it was apperciated by Prof Kostic.

Now I would like to go back to my hostel. With the grants given by the University we established a library which was regularly used by students. Every alternate Sunday we used to get some scholar to come and give a talk. As some of the students had leftist thinking some objections were raised about two magazines, one, Mother India edited by Baburao Patel and the other was Telugu monthly 'Bharathi', a literary magazine, the cover page of which always carried the picture of goddess Saraswati. I got out of the problem of Mother India by confessing that I was getting it to the library because I could not afford it myself. As regards Bharathi many leftists published their writings in that magazine because it was just a literary magazine but the students were not convinced so easily. One day I took Dr C Ramarao who was highly respected progressive intellectual to my hostel on our way home. An active student was there. He took Dr Ramarao aside and enquired about Bharathi. He told him whatever I had being saying all along. The activist told me that Bharathi was welcome because Dr Ramarao told him that even revolutionary poets published their poems in that monthly magazine.

There was another unfortunate incident which was by chance averted. Some students who did not attend the flag-hoisting function on the Independence Day were angry that I did not save the sweets for them to be given later. They had a meeting and decided that they would give me corporal punishment. By then I had got home. One of the peons came home and told my wife that I should not visit the hostel for three or four days. She just understood the opposite and when I came home she said that I was expected in the hostel immediately. Contrary to my practice I somehow did not feel like going that time as I was tired. In the Bible it is rightly said that 'not a sparrow falleth without the heavens knowing it'. Without His consent no one can be punished. Later I met the peon on the road and he reminded me of the advice not to go to the hostel for a few days. After two days of not going there I reasoned that running away from one's duty out of fear would be an act of cowardice. I did not want to brand myself a coward; cautious, yes, though I was. Around 4 pm when the students would be very few in the hostel was the right time for me to visit the hostel. There was only one student who informed me about the anger of the leftists students. It looks as though they had other complaints too. I left the place and later in the evening when I was coming back from the town at about 8 o'clock I started moving to the hostel. Though my reasoning guided me forward the fear did not desert me. My mouth became parched and my tongue was dry as a piece of wood. I entered the hostel and straight went to one of the leaders' room. I had to pretend courage and behave normally. My behaviour should not betray either fear or guilt. I asked for a glass of water. The students are naturally good till circumstances misguide them or demand negative behaviour. All of them started shooting questions. I responded saying: "I am a teacher I'll answer all of your questions but one at a time." One of the students enquired why the sweets I bought with my money were not kept for them. He added that they did not attend the flag hosting because our government was not the people's government. I just corrected them saying that the sweets were brought with the money given by the other warden. This seems to have cooled them. They raised a couple of other points and I cleared the points to their satisfaction. I sincerely believe that workers and students are reasonable till they are provoked by someone or misguided by someone.

There was another incident which is close to my heart because it involves the concept of social justice. An upper caste boy, short, dark, and not so handsome, used castiest language to a tall handsome boy saying, "Pora madigoda" (go away, you cobbler boy). He was actually an ST boy. He gave a good slap to the upper caste fellow. They fought over it and they were taken away to the police station. An intelligent man he was, the circle inspector of station Mr Naidu sent a constable to my house to get me to the station. When I went there the circle inspector told me that it was the Emergency period that he did not have to present them in the court for six months. He added the ST boy had to attend sub-inspector selections the next day. He asked me to effect a compromise. I did and they shook hands and parted. I took the upper caste boy with me and both of us sat on the lawn opposite the hostel. I was audacious in my interlocution: "I am not sure that my caste blood is flowing in my family for last one thousand years. Are you sure that your family has had the same caste blood in last one thousand years." The boy was both realistic and generous: "Well very bitter it is, but true." I always felt that social classification should not lead to hierarchy and wrong behaviour. Sperm has no community, uterus has no community and soul has no community, divinity has no community, nature has no community, planets have no community. Then why should the so called thinking humans think of community identity and misuse it?

While at Osmania, I was invited by the Indian Institute of Advanced Study, Simla, to attend a seminar on social stratification and language behaviour as a discussant. My name was suggested to them by Dr Verma. After going there my teacher advised me also to write a paper which I did and I presented it after a couple of days. Later it was also published as 'A Sociogrammar of Telugu Pronouns'. It is imperative to a teacher to encourage his students to grow academically and it is equally imperative for the students to remember it.

Mr Narothama Reddy was the Vice Chancellor when I joined Osmania. I remember that once I approached him with a letter asking him to start a project which would help Telugu medium students who come to the university strengthen their English. He not only agreed with me but also sent it to the Head of the Department of English for necessary action.

The Osmania University Department of English started an English centre much before the UGC thought of it for other universities.

The Union Public Service Commission invited some university teachers to work in Delhi as Under Secretaries and Deputy Secretaries. My teacher suggested my name for the Under Secretary position. When I was going for the personal talk (interview) Dr Verma gave me two pieces of advice: "Don't be too fast and be composed and slow while answering. When you don't know something please say so. When you don't agree with any of their statements say, 'I beg to differ with you' but don't say I don't agree with you." He added that I should ask for advance increments and if they ask whether it was a condition say, "No, it is just a request." And I went for the interview and Dr Verma's advice was extremely valuable.

I came back. I got the appointment order. I got ready to go. I went to Dr Verma to say good bye. His piece of parting advice reflected his love and care: "I know you drink and I also know that you don't drink when I am around. I appreciate it. Now you are going to Delhi. I won't be there. Be careful. Don't develop a need for drinking." A good teacher thus is a blend of mother's love, father's care, teacher's advice and God's guidance.

Positive attitudes and negative attitudes emanate from one's nature. Nurture strengthens them though sometimes it may disturb too. Culture has its own role to play in this context. The teachers who helped me to grow, the friends who strengthened my existential fibre and the administrators who buoyed my career all were independent of any sectarian criteria. All were supportive to me because of their positive attitude of life and their positive assessment of my calibre. This applies to the international linguistic community and also the publishers who published my books were helpful in building my academic and cognizant personality.

Let's be clear about one thing: no two people are alike. As we have said that there are about 144,000 types of people. We will go into some details of this concept.

Human beings are identified by their race, language, creed, caste and gender besides physical correlates like height and weight. More important will be the classification in terms of their nature which gets moulded by the nurture they get. An individual's initiative and his or her response to a given situation are conditioned by their **svabhava** (nature) and nurture provides the **prabhava** (acculturation).

If one takes the twenty-seven stars each one with its four feet (pada), we get 108 tracks of birth. Besides, the lagna of the individual and the placement of different planets in the zodiac signs will indicate the prognosis of their life.

Victor Cohn reported in the Indian Express (Hyderabad, 22/8/1999) that a research team at John Hopkins University (USA) identified three basic personality types—Alpha, Beta and Gamma. Alpha humans are 'cautious, equable or steady, well-oriented'. They take a comprehensive view of things, adjust to new situation gradually and are self-dependent. Betas are 'generally rapid, bright, and clever, blithe, light-hearted'. They are not worried about the future. They adapt well and are not demanding but they are 'articulate in voicing what they do ask'. Gammas are 'irregular and uneven, often brilliant, yet either over-cautious or under-cautions, over-demanding or under-demanding'. They are 'moody, often mixed and confused before adjusting to new situations'. They 'take in too much or too little' and 'hold on for too long', 'they are either well in focus or far out of focus'.

The Homoeopathic philosophy talks of three chronic Miasma-Psora, Syphilis and Psychosis. James Kent puts it succinctly (1900): "The internal state of man is prior to that which surrounds him; therefore, environment is not cause; it is only, as it were, a sounding board; it only reacts upon and reflects the internal... Diseases... are but the outward expression of man's interiors."

The Miasmatic undertone of a person may be a single Miasm or a combination of two or three Miasms. The Psoric person is said to be inquisitive and basically optimistic. The Sycotic person is said to be cautious and secretive. The Syphilitic person is said to be easily trusting and also easily driven to desperation.

The Bhagavad Gita talks of three gunas (traits)—Sattva, Rajas, and Tamas. Knowledge or intelligence is the indicator of Sattva. Inspirational tendency is the indicator of Rajas. Idleness, confusion and blind acceptance indicate Tamas. All humans have in them these gunas in different proportions and one of them dominates at a given time.

No doubt the genes determine the basic svabhava. But there is something more important we cannot ignore. If people born under a star belonging to Mesha, Simha and Dhanush rashis (constellations) are observed to take interest in management, administration and armed forces, we see something common to all of them: **authority**. If people born under a star belonging to Vrishabha, Kanya and Makara rasis take interest in wealth creation and money management, marketing and business houses, we will see that **wealth** plays critical role in their thinking. If people born under a star belonging to Mithuna, Tula and Kumbha rasis take special interest in helping others and guiding others, we can see that their focus is on **service**. If people born under a star belonging to Karkataka, Vrishchika and Meena rashis take interest in growing on their own with the help of knowledge, devotion and set norms, we can say they are guided by **self-direction** where self is both physical and spiritual. Such generalization may not hold good all the time because, the lagna of one's birth and the placement of planets in different zodiac signs also have their role to play.

The four groupings mentioned above are shown as varnas in some books. Here the varna is cosmic and astral where as caste is mundane and societal which plays no role in deciding the basic type of a human being. Whatever be the genetic predisposition, astral orientation or environmental influence, an individual can turn the tide of his basic nature with God's grace. God here is paramatma who brooks no differences. One can with effort turn one's mind in a new direction and achieve success with the help of divine grace. The divine grace`is mediated by a Guru, who can be an Avadhuta like Sri Ramadutha Swami, a Sant Mahatma, a teacher, a friend, a parent or even a spouse.

Syed Mehamod Ali was Joint Registrar (ACCTS) of Osmania university. He was by nature a friendly person and my relationship with him was because of my wardenship. Besides he had visited Rehamatabad (Ananthasamudram peta) in Nellore district. That Darga was not very far from my village and my muncle was a staunch devote of Hazarath (In Telugu we say adarattayya).

In 1977 June I left for Delhi. I went with my family. I was given a send off at the railway station by my kith and kin and friends including my closest friend BJ Premasagar who came all the way from Guntur to see me off. I reached Delhi and from the railway station we hired a taxi to Janakpuri where I had already hired a house. On the way we picked up two cots for our new accommodation. It was in the C-sector of Janakpuri. The upper floor of an independent house belonged to Shri CS Kohli, a bank branch manager and a very friendly and helpful person. The next day I went and reported to duty at the UPSC. The first fortnight was for acclimatization, which helped me to understand the intricacies of one of the most important constituent bodies of India.

Here I want to relate a strange incident. I was given a room which was not properly cleaned and the fan was not working. I waited for a week and wrote a letter to the Under Secretary (Housekeeping). I offered to clean the room myself if I was given a broom. The housekeeping section came immediately and saw the whole place and sent a boy to clean it up. Here is an interesting twist. That boy started grumbling saying that he does not belong to the caste which cleans up cobwebs and sweep the floor. I consoled him saying that I was a Brahmin (Bhumihar Brahmin) but I would not be unhappy to clean the room. I asked him to handover the broom to me. He was kind enough to politely say no and condescended to clean up the room. A couple of days later the fan was replaced. A similar incident had taken place when I was at Osmania. The Department of Linguistics had been shifted to an independent building near the Law College. I was given the last room in the ground floor and adjacent to it was the gent's toilet. Once the toilet cleaner was absent for a few days and its stink was unbearable. I spent more than half an hour cleaning it up. Then I sent a letter to the Principal of the Arts College about the situation and how I tackled it. Professor G Rami Reddy the Principal and Prof J Satyanarayana of Commerce Department appreciated my Gandhian stand and immediately sent someone to set it right.

I got my daughters admitted to the Andhra Educational Society school of Janakpuri and my son was admitted into the Andhra Educational Society Middle school in Karol Bagh. These schools had an interesting practice: the teachers would explain the subject first in Telugu and then in English. Shri Burra Venkatappaiah was the chairman of the Andhra Educational society. Srimathi Ramadevi of Law Ministry was associated with society. The office of the AES was in the High school situated in Deendayal Upadhyaya Marg formerly called Rouse Avenue. I was made Chairman of the Academic Standards Committee and I conducted many special seminars for the teachers of AES schools.

Dr Venkatappaya was also the Chairman of Rural Electrification Corporation. One day the corporation secretary said the he was going to Nellore the following week to approve electrification of four villages. I asked him to include my village in this list. He got the details from me, visited Nellore and did the needful. My experience in the UPSC where I saw some IAS officers coming as Under Secretaries and Deputy Secretaries made me appreciate the work done by officers to keep the civilised societies going on the right track.

Professor Daswani of JNU told me that Punjabi University, Patiala was interested in getting me there as a reader of department of Anthropological Linguistics. The Department was headed by Professor HS Gill, an internationally known semiotician. My paper on stylistics published in Indian Journal of Applied Linguistics caught his attention and that paper became the base for my interview which was held at the office of Association of Indian Universities in Delhi. The journal was published by US Bahri, a good friend and a scholarly publisher.

My stay in Delhi had two distinct contributions to my mindset. Besides the respect for administrators and the incorruptible ethos of UPSC the two cities of Delhi and New Delhi (NCR) give us a broad picture of India, as represented in Delhi, which has two major segments of population: the Hindusthani speaking and Punjabi speaking. As part of my work I visited Varanasi and also Hyderbad to conduct examinations. My wife had an interesting remark to make. She thought I should not visit any shrines without her. So she thought I should not visit Kashi Vishwanath Temple in Varanasi because I was going there alone. As a 'husband-in-love-with-wife' I agreed with her, I followed it everywhere. She did not follow this advice. She visited Vaishnodevi temple with her brother and daughter and without me. Might be wife includes husband, but not the other way round.

I am a very strange fellow when it comes to being right. The landlord let me the house on a rent of 450 rupees per month whereas its market value was rupees 550 per month. I was feeling guilty so l started looking for a cheaper flat which it seems he had smelt. One day he called me into his drawing room enquired whether I was looking for a flat and if so, why. I told him that I was feeling guilty of under paying the rent. This was sometime in June 1978. He laughed and wondered whether his wife or anyone else mentioned about the inadequate rent. I said it was my own mindset problem. He said that there was no need to feel guilty and no need of more rent. I offered to raise the rent by 25 rupees in the month of July because I was to get an increment of 50 rupees. He smiled and said: "I am not asking for it. That's your problem." This mindset doesn't seem to me totally idiosyncratic. Recently I heard a nephew of mine did the same thing in Chennai and a puncle of mine did the same thing in Srikalahasti. It looks like the mindset of our clan.

Our shifting to Patiala is still confusing, amusing and amazing to me. We shifted to Patiala in the month of December 1978. And we put all our luggage in a truck and my four children were seated on the seats behind the driver's seat. We put all the luggage and our beds and other things in the body of the truck. We made ourselves comfortable on the beds and used blankets to protect ourselves from the December cold. I think we started from Delhi at 5 pm and reached Patiala at 9 pm. The landlord's brother-in-law kept tea ready for us and also got us dinner. The proverbial Punjabi hospitality started the very first day. In the first week of January we went to Senior Modern Higher Secondary School for admissions. My daughters did well though the last child who was four years old gave a blank answer sheet because the whole thing was new to her. Then I took my son to Our Lady Fathima School where he was admitted after a lot of coaxing and requesting. The two schools were the good schools around beside the more famous Yadavendra Public School. My eleven and a half years' stay in Patiala—first seven and half as Reader and last four years as Professor—was remarkable from an academic point of view. Several dozens of researchers got their MPhils and PhDs in the area of stylistics. I was Head of the Department twice. I published several books and articles while at Patiala. In 1985 I went to the University of Illinois at Urbana-Champaign and the University of California at Berkeley as a Fulbright Fellow. I worked on a project of Literary Semantics for which I took a poem of Robert Frost, a stanza of Rabindranath Tagore's Gitanjali and a soliloquy of Hamlet for readers' response. While at Urban-Champaign Prof Braj Kachru and Yamuna Kachru were of great help. While at Berkeley (2 weeks) I was a guest of Tom Williams who welcomed me and hosted me because Professor Som P Ranchan of Himachal University, Simla, had requested him to have me. I have got to mention my meeting with the famous Comparative Dravidian Specialist MB Emeneau. In our conversation he said that I would have been speaking to him in French had the French defeated the British in Battle of Plassey. I blurted out with, "Thank God British won it." He asked me why, and I said it. I very happily replied, "Shakespeare". He responded: "Don't say that to a Frenchman." He raised his arms and said, "O Moliére". My non-smart brain did not realize that I was speaking to a Frenchman. Any how we finished our lunch and he took me home and gave me a copy of the new edition of his Dravidian Etymological Dictionary. I came home and related that incident to my host Tom Williams. Many of us cannot identify the ethnic background of Americans on the basis of their surnames. Tom Williams my host was of Welsh background. He said that Emeneau was a Frenchman and hence the feelings about Plassey. I remember watching an episode of Andy Williams show on the TV. Andy Williams was asked about his nationality. He said, "Of course American". The other character said, "Oh no but your real nationality", and his reply was Welsh. This sub-nationality feeling is not that easily forgettable because of the surnames. Sometimes these names are also used for enjoying humour. Edward Heath and James Callaghan were Prime Ministers of Great Britain at different times. Once Edward Heath said, "James Callaghan is very clever. He is an Englishman with an Irish surname contesting a Welsh seat." In America the Irishmen called themselves micks and have a sense of solidarity. This sub-nationality consciousness is not unnatural but people living in a country should archive it for wider consciousness and cultivate the spirit of nationalism. In India specially because of different parameters of identity like caste, creed, region, language, divisions and sub divisions are too many. That's why

Dr Ambedkar advised people to inculcate the national spirit.

An interesting aspect of a community identity is its food habits. For example makki di roti and sarso (n) da sag remind us of Punjab, Shrikhand reminds of Maharastra. Pesarattu (a dosa of moongdal), gongura and avakaya remind us of the Andhras, avial of the Malayalis and Pulikolambu of the Tamilians. My host took me to a restaurant called Pasand in Berkeley. In the menu card I saw the name Pesarattu and I asked the waiter whether it was a Telugu restaurant and the answer was yes.

In my absence for a year my wife and children were in Hyderabad with my parents. They moved out to Hyderabad just before the Operation Bluestar and then returned to Patiala in April 1985 and my wife took care of the admissions of the students. My son already was there in Ludhiana doing his BTech in Agricultural Engineering in Punjab Agricultural University. By the first week of the June I was back in Patiala.

Somewhere in 1984 I was offered a Professorship at Manipur University. I went to my Vice Chancellor to seek his advice. I was active as Head of the Department so he took it for granted that I was already Professor. He was so gracious to say that there was a post vacant in the department. I could apply for it after I came back from my Fulbright stay in the USA.

Now that I was back the post was advertised and the interviews were fixed but postponed. Meanwhile a new Vice Chancellor took over. Actually he was Vice Chancellor earlier and he came back for the second time. He was in jail after Operation Bluestar on a trumped up charge because he had condemned the Operation Bluestar. I visited him while in jail. This visit of mine he remembered when he came back as Vice Chancellor. In no time the post was advertised again, interviews were held in 1986, and I got the promotion.

Punjab has much to offer to reconstruct the history. This is part of Sapthasindu where Vedas were composed. Punjabi as a language is close to Sanskrit, in certain aspects of sound patterns and the use of lexical items. For a Patialavi like me

Captain Amarendhra Singh, Maharaja of Patiala, was a person to remember. While referring to the gender system of Punjabi I used to say Dudh (milk) and pani (water) would remain masculine whereas chai (tea) and coffee would remain feminine and even the Maharaja of Patiala would not be able to break the rule. I cannot resist the temptation to say that Punjabis are famous for giving interesting names to their children. It becomes easy among Sikhs because they will add Singh to men, Kaur for women. The most fascinating name I would never forget is Gumdur Singh (depression distancer); he was a BDO at that time. I had a friend Inderjit Singh Jeyji who was the muncle of maharaja. His surname has a history. These were the people who refused to pay the beard tax (jijiya). These are a subgroup of Shergills who are a subgroup of Gills. Similarly Brars are the subgroups of Siddhus. Sometimes some of these names are difficult to identify for outsiders. For example Khera is a Khatri whereas Khaira is a Jat. I would like to add an interesting perceptual differential. 15 August, 1947 is remembered as Independence Day and we generally say before Independence and in Punjab we commonly hear the expression 'before partition' and 'after partition'.

Some of the businessmen (baniya) in Punjab look like Telugu Vaishyas, a vegetarian community which specializes in business and who are supposed to be strong in mathematics. This I was told when I was in Delhi. My neighbour Gupta was talking about his son's weak command of English. He casually mentioned he was strong in mathematics but it was not a big deal because mathematics was in their blood. This kind of propensity of a community to excel in a skill can be questioned but can also be taken up for empirical investigation. It is said our genes carry with them the nature of our forefathers. We may mention also here the (Telugu) Vaishyas are generally said to lack a particular enzyme (pseudo cholinesterase). My life in Patiala was made fruitful and enjoyable by friends like Dr Puar, Dr GB Singh, Dr Chanchal Singh and also the Doctors of the Rajendra Medical College and Hospital, where

Professor Tyagi, Dr Bhasin, Dr Jindal and Pyaremohan were of great help.

The expansion of my knowledge is of paramount importance. Semiotics as a discipline got widespread recognition in Punjab thanks to the efforts of Professor HS Gill, an internationally known semiotician and linguist trained in USA and France. He would believe in the students developing their own cognizance instead of copy-pasting what others say. He always told his students that he was more interested in finding out what they think about the given topic and not what others think of it. This got special recognition from the examiners and scholars who used to say our theses were much more original than those of other departments. Now I cannot look at any text written, spoken or presented on the screen without bringing in the semiotic tools of syntactic organization, semantic signification and pragmatic evaluation.

While at Patiala I got a major project to prepare an Encyclopaedia of Linguistics with two Postdoctoral scholars to work on it. Dr Imtiaz Hasnain and Dr Vijay Kaul worked on this project. It was later brought out by Allied Publishers by 2007. They also published Semantic Theories and Language Teaching by Anvita Abbi and myself. Punjabi University published my Linguistic Spectrum. A local publisher brought out my Stylistics of Poetry. Sinare Kavita Riti (C Narayana Reddy's Poetic Style) Bhasha Vyasalu (Lingusitcs Songs) and Gitaganam (Gita in lyrical form) are the three books that were published in Telugu. Thus my academic life at Patiala was very productive. In April 1990 I shifted to Central Institute of English and Foreign Languages (CEFL now EFLU) as a Professor in the Department Distance Education.

My first few days at Hyderabad were a little lost because I was missing Punjab. Slowly I got used to it with its cosmopolitan icing of a Telugu cake. The seventeen years stint at CIEFL was again very satisfying in many respects. The very first good thing I did was to raise objection to a paltry amount being

paid as daily wages, the same amount which was paid in 1976 in Osmania hostels. Similarly with great effort I could get a homeo physician at CIEFL health centre. Starting with a one month Summer Institute in Functional Linguistics in honour of Dr SK Verma I started the tradition of hosting self-financing seminars and conferences. In 1997 I attended an International Systemic Functional Congress at Cardiff. Here is a photo which I had with Prof Michael Halliday and Prof Christian Matthiessen.

Under the expansive influence of Professor Talgeri the Vice Chancellor we conducted the first International Congress on English Grammar in 1998. This ICEG has travelled to Hong Kong, the Philippines and different parts of India so far. It is during this period I did my LLB (Osmania), LLM (Kakatiya) and PhD in Law (Nalsar 2013). I was 70 when I got this second doctorate. I always quoted it to say age is no bar for studies. It may be for getting married again.

It may not be out of place to mention a distinction achieved by me in 1992. The International Biographical Center of Cambridge nominated me as International Man of the year for 1992–1993. The newspapers widely reported it and Doordarshan TV interviewed me in this regard.

I was ardent admirer of the Bhagavad Gita. I started reading Mahabaratha in Telugu by Pilaka Ganapathi Sastri published in the Sunday edition of a news paper, when I was barely thirteen. Similarly I started reading Bhagavad Gita at the age of sixteen. I brought a copy of the Gita Press English edition at Kakinada Railway station where I had gone to participate in an elocution competition on behalf of my college in Nellore. In 1985 I published a condensed version of the Gita in lyrical form. Later it was sung by Mr Bhim Shankar, a disciple of Nukala Satyanarayana. The music was composed by Mosalikanti Saratchandra Kumar and his co-composer Dr Seshulatha. A cassette was released and a live concert of this Gitaganam was given in October 2001 at Gokak Auditorium, CIEFL. I always said that the Bhagavad Gita is a social treatise on spiritual socialism and detached attachment. This was covered by the newspaper Hindu in great detail in its Metro Plus issue of November 1, 2001.

I was Dean of English Studies when Professor Talgeri was Vice Chancellor and we were successful in reorganizing the Institute into schools. Technically I retired in 2005 and I was reemployed for two years and finally I quit in 2007.

For about three years (2002–2004), I was sent to Lucknow as the Director of the Regional centre of CIEFL. It was a wonderful experience of strengthening the centre and also in practising what is called elite leadership which guides but allows full freedom to colleagues to grow on their own terms and conditions. I practised all the good things Dr Verma taught me by his own behaviour. I was never late to office and I never took any undue advantage of my office. I was very particular to pay for my personal telephone calls and personal use of staff car. As we had the first ICEG Hyderabad in 1998, we had International Systemic Functional Congress at Lucknow in 2003. Both were very successful in terms of attendance, scholarly presence and hospitality. In 1998 hotels like Hotel Golkonda, Amrita Castle and Raj Classic Inn housed our delegates. We had a grand dinner hosted by Orient Longmans at Grand Kakatiya. Similarly in 2003 Lucknow hotels housed our delegates and took care of them. So many publishers, business persons, banks helped us in conducting the self-financing programme in Hyderabad and Lucknow.

The International Systemic Functional Grammar Congress was attended by many important linguists working within the theory of systemic grammar: MAK Halliday, Ruquaiya Hassan, Robin Fawcett, James Martin, Christian Matthiessen besides many of my Indian colleagues working in the model.

Professor Ganeshan, Prof Dimri and Prof Sastri as Vice Chancellors at different times were a great help to me. As Dean of English Studies I had wonderful cooperation of Mr Baburao the Section officer and his staff like Ms Padma. This cooperation of the Registrars, Dr Jayashankar, Dr Venkateswara Rao, at different times was very helpful. I would like to make a special mention of Mr Balakrishna Rao who was a section officer in the Department of Distance Education and later in administrative section. I specially remember with respect the way he expressed his objection to my being late to the academic council meeting.

3

My mother reared me. I roared. My wife geared me. A baby girl woke up on 1–10–1950 around 11 am. This was in a hospital at Nellore. 'Around' is significant because the head coming out was followed by the use of forceps to bring the baby out. As a result there was the problem with the identification of birth star 'Anuradha' or 'Jyeshtha'. Finally it was identified as Anuradha. She was the daughter of Amancherla Natarajan who was the brother-in-law of a paunt of mine. He was a permanent resident of Hyderabad. Her mother was Ms A Ramaratnam, a daughter of Dubagunta Subrahmanyam and Kanakamma of Indukurupet of Nellore district. The baby girl was named Rajyalakshmi. She lost her mother when she was about three years old. She was brought up by her MGM and PGM. She was in Nellore with her PGM for her school education. I was in Nellore doing my BA at VR College. She was about nine years old and I was sixteen and half when I really saw her. That was it. There was no going back. It was an unbelievable, totally 'mental' and might be 'spiritual' attachment. I used to visit them almost daily to say hello to all of them but actually to see her. She used to visit with her PGM the local temples every evening, the temples of Hanuman, Subrahmanyaswami and Saibaba. I also used to visit the same temples off Grand Trunk Road. Her grandmother would be looking at the idols and praying. We also did it but we did more of 'preying' on each other for 'looks'. The age was such that not one would understand what was happening but it went on. One day in their house she was up on the terrace looking down at me and I was down looking up at her. We were totally locked in those looks. Her grandmother's sister noticed it and said to her elder sister: "Akka, that girl and this boy are totally lost in looking at each other. Might be they will get married." It was evening and the evening angels must have said amen. We got married in 1965 on my birthday June 24. She had finished her 9th class and I finished my MA in English and also I finished one year of teaching. She was going to be fifteen and I was 22. After marriage she shifted to Hyderabad and stayed for a while with her parents. Her step-mother has always being very kind to her and helpful to her. My wife was with me in Nagpur only for a few months. Then I shifted to Hyderabad and we were together in Hyderabad, we were in the UK together, in Delhi together, in Patiala together and in Lucknow together. We have long innings of togetherness, extremely pleasant, I can vouch for myself. My children—Gautam, Sujatha, Maithili and Himabindu think that I was dominating, however loving I might be, and as a result she did not bloom to her best.

Before my son was born in June 1967 she had a miscarriage. While at Nagpur, a Telugu speaking tribal soothsayer told me that I got a playful cobra couple killed when they were in water. This happened in 1961. He asked me to atone for it and I did it. When she was carrying my son another tribal soothsayer said that a disembodied soul was disturbing her. This he said when my mother asked him whether there was a ghost in the house. He said that my wife had gone out to see a movie in a hall built close to a burial ground, after she washed her hair but did not oil it. The soul entered her with the help of her dry hair. He correctly said that my mother was dreaming of my wife jumping up around with dishevelled hair. My mother said that it was true. He suggested a spiritual remedy. We followed it. He wanted me to give him a gold ring after the birth of my son. I agreed. He came back and collected the ring. In 1968 November my second child Sujatha was born. From about March of 1968 my wife had developed twitching of hands followed by pregnancy hysteria. She was wonderfully treated by Dr N Ramaiah, a great homeopath who used to come from Chikkadpally, Hyderabad. The medicines that mainly helped her were Tarentula, Hyoscyamus, Arnica and Sulphur. For delivery we went to my puncle's place in Machilipatnam, coastal Andhra Pradesh.

This has led me to a regular study of homeopathy which culminated in my appearing for RMP (H) exams in 1975. So I became a Registered Medical Practitioner too.

My wife again conceived in 1969 and immediately the twitching symptom returned. It was successfully treated by the homeopath. The third child was born in England in 1970. As I could not think of a good name associated with Buddha, we gave her the name Maithili, chosen by my wife. She was a great Rama bhakta. In England we had to register the birth with the name of baby within forty days of birth. Again later in October, 1973 our fourth child was born. This time the name associated with Buddhism was suggested by Dr Meenakshi the daughter of Professor Bh Krishnamurti. One son followed by three daughters, my wife thought that was enough. With the help of her mother, she underwent tubectomy in 1973 itself.

All through our stay in India we were a full family with several others staying with us besides the six of us. As a result our mind was always full and positive, never empty and negative. Ketu in the seventh house of my horoscope 'guaranteed' her ill health but manageable because of other planets like Guru, Sukra aspecting Ketu in the seventh house. Result is ill health which was wonderfully managed by good doctors and their staff, her own will power, and my careful attendance. She was hospitalised at least 35 times and I never allowed her to be served by anyone else.

In 1981 she underwent finger-valvotomy at PGI Chandigarh to take care of her mitral stenosis. Dr Suri was the surgeon and she was mainly looked after by my mother-in-law and I made myself available all the time. The two medicines I remembered she regularly used after operation were Lasix and Lanoxin, accompanied by Pot Klor syrup. We used to visit PGI once a month on a Wednesday. On one Wednesday the doctor asked me to take some weight off her because I was slim. This hurt her. After that she started dieting vigorously. This was repeat of what had happened in UK. While on a picnic my wife saw an

American lady, a little huge, taking only tomato and a cheese piece. She mumbled in Telugu about her food with a question mark and I told her she was dieting. My wife herself was a little big as she put on weight after her delivery in April 1970. She was ten stones (140 pounds). She came home and started dieting with strictly a plate of rice per meal and slimcea bread. I think within a few months she came down to 8 stones (112 pounds). Her desire to do things which were needed was very strongly aided by her willpower. While in Patiala she used to do an hour of Yoga to keep herself trim and active. She used to cook a lot and make delectable dishes. We also enjoyed one year stay in a huge bungalow called X-en house with a huge kitchen garden with many fruit trees. For sometime my mother stayed with us and she was very happy with the house. From there we moved to the Teg Bahadur Bungalow in Lehal, again a big house. It was from here in 1981 we went to the PGI. My father-in-law and mother-in-law came and the latter took care of her during her hospitalization. It is from here we noticed that my first daughter and brother-in-law (AV Ravindarnath) starting exchanging letters. It culminated in their wedding in 1984. My daughter had just finished her first year of her college in Patiala. After marriage she did privately MA in English, MA in Astrology and MA in music (sitar). She is now a mother of two and PGM of two grand-daughters.

My son joined Escorts in Bangalore after his BTech (Ag Eng) which he did at Punjab Agricultural University, Ludhiana. There he chose a Tamil speaking life partner, Kavitha, the daughter of an Air Vice Marshal. They got married in 1993. They have a son who has now become a successful theatre artist as predicted by my father.

The next daughter got married in 1994 to Mr Badri Prasad an auditor in Banglaore. Now she is mother of two college going kids. Her son Dhruva who shares my lagna (Karkataka) bamboozled me by coming out with a sentence of grammatical metaphor, as a counter example to my statement that pronouns cannot be modified. "The Sleeping me was woken up by a she." He was also the one who made me realise that the present perfect is perfect+present: in other words 'has come' is equal to 'come+is'. My daughter is now associated with Ashwasan, a spiritual healing organization in Bangalore. She did her MA in English in Patiala.

The last daughter did her MA in Sociology with distinction from Osmania University. Later she did MA in English privately. She has recently done an in-service BEd programme. She got married in 1998 to I. Venkatesh. She is now a mother of two daughters. One of the daughters who shares my birth star Purvabhadra (Praharshita) has added to my linguistic terminology. Expressions used for greeting and establishing cordiality she called 'pleasing' language, whereas information-sharing or information-seeking sentences 'telling language'. In linguistics the pleasing language is called 'phatic communion'. The other granddaughter or both of them I don't remember who exactly came out with an interesting statement: 'God is a concept. Once you give it a form the concept is reinforced'. All this they did when they were school children.

The pride: Me, She and the Cubs that sprang off

All these wonderful things happened in spite of frequent hospitalizations of my ever-smiling wife. She was admitted in

NIMS in 1992 for hernia correction but ended up with also Double Valve Replacement (Mitral valve and Aortic valve) St Judes valves were in her body till 26 January 2018, the day of her liberation and my lonesomeness. This lonesomeness brings back to my memory Keats's lines which have ever been my favourite lines (Ode to Nightingale):

'My heart aches and a drowsy numbers
Pains my sense as though of hemlock I had drunk…
I am half in love with death...'

The surgeon who did her DVR was Dr Satyanarayana, a student of Dr Suri of PGI. And his excellent treatment and my wife's willpower saw her in good stead. Dr Venkata Reddy assisted the chief surgeon. She was brought back from ICCU to private room without going through the recovery ward. My forty days' stay in the hospital was the beginning of my uninterrupted service. Her cardiological follow up was taken care up by Dr Padmanabham who was first in Mahaveer hospital, later KIMS. It is during the DVR operation that I used to regularly pray to Puttaparthi Saibaba. Later in 1996 she underwent hysterectomy and also hernia correction once again. This was at Kamineni hospital, a very nice visitable building it is housed in.

Keeping the distance and the relationship between my University and CGHS recognised-hospitals we shifted to Care Hospitals. On the advice of Dr Suryaprakash we visited Care Hospital, Secunderabad, which we got so much used to because of the doctor and the sisters like Jessy, we used to call this hospital our holiday retreat.

Somewhere in 2008 an astrologer told me that September 29, 2008 was a bad day for her and if she survived it 15–5–2009 would be her final day. I decided to fight it, for which I wanted to go 'beyond science'. I invited a Purohit, Shri Kommu Bhanumurthy, and asked him to do puja every day at home, by doing abhisheka with Panchamrutham (cow milk, cow milk curd, cow ghee, honey and jagri, or unrefined sugar) followed by mruthyunjaya mantram repeated 27 times. The day came; 29 September she was short of breath. I took her to hospital and the 2D echo showed that one valve was stuck. Dr Surya Prakash immediately put her on special medicine to open it. I visited a nearby Shirdi Saibaba temple and I prayed to him to extend her life by taking 5 years off my life. By afternoon she was back to normal. After a couple of days we came home. From then onwards it was continuous monitoring of BP, saturation point (availability of oxygen in the body) and pulse rate besides glucose levels. 15-5-2009 we were in hospital again. My body was disturbed and my brother was disturbed in Bangalore and asked my sister whether there was any problem. It looks as though in the absence of our parents the eldest son gets a kind of vibratory responsibility. Our granddaughter in Syracuse, USA had a disturbing dream too. I was praying to Baba. The valve was not stuck and it was only a pulse rate variation problem. Later three times the valve was stuck, twice she was treated at Care Hospital, Nampally and the fourth time she was treated at Narayana Hrudayala, Bangalore. The cardiologists who attended on her were excellent. Dr Suryaprakash cut down on medicines to help her be a bit more active. Her diabetes, BP, pulse rate problem, needed anticoagulation were taken care of well. She also underwent electric shock to control her pulse rate. Homeopathy was there to help us.

The care she got at the Secunderabad Care Hospital was indeed exemplary. The expertise of Dr Suryaprakash and his colleagues assisted by the nursing staff led by Sister Jessy, Sister Swaroopa and Nutritionist Sunitha and guided by the administrative staff led by Major Nageswararao, and assisted by Ms Radha and others were always remembered by my wife, me and other relatives. The kind of exhuberance she showed after coming back from a bout of hospitalization speaks well of the treatment and also the morale boosting attendance. Here is a photograph of the queen, immediately after coming from the hospital, to illustrate my point.

For one of her birthdays we went to Tirupati and participated in Venkateswara Kalyanam. We also prayed to both Venkateswaraswami and Saibaba for another three years.

My brother Dr Narasimha Rao and his wife Dr Puspalatha, both homeopaths, did their bit. Actually my brother was both a doctor and counsellor. He used to say before her and after her that all my post MA degrees I got after marrying her and thus she can be considered a great supporter if not my mentor. Dr Padma, a cousin of mine helped her with the services of a psychiatrist. Dr Rebecca Priyadarshini a naturopath was a great help too.

The next year we could not go to Tirupati and we had Srinivasa kalyanam at home. All these were done to see that her willpower did not weaken. I remember about seven or eight years ago we bought a saree, Arundhati silk saree, paying seventeen thousand rupees by my credit card to boost her morale. Actually this is also due to my weak money management abilities. This should not be understood that I wasted her money too. No. She inherited a house in Indukurupet as a gift from her maternal grandmother. Any wealth from wife's relatives cannot be used by others.The Manusmriti says it, and the Quran says it. Only she could use it and give it to her daughters. When my son was doing Agricultural Engineering I used about Rs 22,000 of that money for his BTech. Much later on an occasion when he got the money by selling a piece of land in Hyderabad, he gave her one lakh rupees on my advice. She gave that money to her daughters. I used to maintain a kind of parity among my daughters whenever I gave them gifts. Finally she sold a piece of land for about 2.7 lakhs and gave fifty thousand rupees to each daughter and fifty thousand to our son's son, twenty-thousand to the temple built by my last puncle with the support of many of us. In this context I can say that with different publishers' help I could do many great things like donating libraries to different schools. This I did through my Divine Humanism Trust.

Using a credit card a little foolishly was common with me. One day I borrowed fifteen hundred rupees from the Standard Charted Bank using the card and immediately spent five hundred rupees on a dictionary. I came home. My wife saw the dictionary and gave very soft and sweet snub: "You borrowed fifteen hundred and spent five hundred rupees on a dictionary? Might be you need it." This made me realize where all money was going. So far I gave away several hundreds of books to different libraries. But I am still left with several hundreds of books.

After eight years were over, I prayed for another year. My wife developed lung infection most probably from the food plates of the train we were travelling by from Bangalore to Hyderabad. She had developed some mental disturbance because of sleeping pills. That medicine was immediately stopped and first a neurologist was consulted and later a psychiatrist. She took a small tablet for mental disturbance which corrected it but led to too much weight of the lower part of the body. Some other factors like lack of walking exercise must have contributed to her problem. Finally it was the bed sore that did her in. Serious radical treatment could not be given because of the heart condition. Finally she was in hospital for 15 days for vac therapy, etc. I prayed to Baba saying he could decide her longevity but requested him to see that she maintained reasonable health. On the 25th of January we came home with vac therapy continuing and b-bap help continuing. Next day our son came from Chennai gave her food followed by medicine. He told her that the medicines were given by me. She asked for me, I just peeped into the room and she saw me that was the last flickering of looks and no locking of looks. She went to sleep and in her sleep she slept off. I wanted to go to the book exhibition. I went to her and tried to wake her up to tell her about the book exhibition. But no response. This is ten days after my prayer to Baba.

The fifty-three years we spent as spouses were for me splendidly happy years. Splendid it was and happy it was because notwithstanding health problems and money problems life went on happily glancing, smiling, caressing, lipping, biting, pressing, and spousing. My daughter-in-Law, Kavitha, rightly said that my wife had not given me just happiness, but gave me BLISS. Absolutely correct. I certainly would like to agree with my sister, Sailaja, that my nature was such to effect that situation. For someone who is in love with his wife what else is happiness. A younger brother of mine once called me 'mental' which I think he wanted to mean to say that I was 'foolishly generous and ridiculously trusting'. I would like to say he was not wrong because I think profusion of ideas leads to confusion awaiting fusion. When I used the phrase splendidly happy years it only reflected my subjective perception of my life. Some existential facts, others may say, could not be considered either splendid or happy. I have a very peculiar habit of generalising and sermonising. Happiness is the positive response of an individual to a given situation. The gap between what we expect and what we get decides our happiness. If someone doesn't expect too much he is easily contented with what he gets and the happiness is the result. Similarly I always say let's follow 'no credit no debit policy' which means we are not responsible for our success or for our failure. Only we are responsible for our efforts and consequences. Once we accept this, our failure does not disturb us. Let me take the cases where I went for interview but was not successful. It so happened wherever I was not taken someone better was taken or no one was taken. The only place where I was not selected because I used a wrong English expression ('minor games' for 'indoor games') was a public school. This also I took was to my advantage because within two years I went to UK for my PhD.

Many of us don't accept our weaknesses and we want to get things whether we really deserve them or not. I will not be unhappy to accept that I suffer from self love. When Jesus Christ said, 'Love they neighbour as thyself' this positive feeling about oneself is mandated. Otherwise I can't explain how I loved every place I stayed at, whether as a student or as a teacher—Kullur, Nellore, Nagpur, Lucknow, Delhi, Patiala, Hyderabad, York, Urbana-Champaign. Any disadvantage I faced I take it as not worth-remembering, let alone harbouring any ill will. Well, this kind of love for the people you meet and the places you stay at is I think an instance of sentimentality. I do get attached to people and even to things but not much to money or position. Well, sentimentality is no doubt a sort of mental phenomenon. Here is an Encore coffee cup I bought at York in 1970. I keep it and I use it occasionally.

A sister of mine once said I was judgemental. We need lot of thinking to do self-analysis and we also need moral courage to accept our weaknesses.

Being deeply in love with one's own wife actually opens up a question: what do we mean by love? Love as a concept is as difficult to define as God. This non-definability I experienced in the last two years of our being together. This word love we find in the English version of the Bible has several words in the original Greek version: agape (unconditional love or natural love like God's love); eros (love between a man and woman); philios (brotherly love); storge (familiar love); ludus (playful love); mania (oppressive love); pragma (enduring love); philautia (self love). How can we decide whether a feeling is mere attraction, infatuation, or selfless love? That's why non-definability is a part of our cognizance. When we communicate that question-begging remains. That's why we hear expressions like 'I didn't mean it', 'Well, actually what I meant was'. This generally goes under the concept of deconstruction.

Now and then I used to tease my wife saying mine was pure love (might be agape), hers was possessive love, a combination of eros and philautia. Let's be clear that there is no certainty in the area of non-definable concepts. My wife's answer always was may be, with a wonderful smile. Her smile, her strong willpower and her ability to respond retortingly was fabulous. Not 'to retort' does not mean 'no relishable repartee'. I once said her 'hoof' was a little too strong. Her birth star (Anuradha) animal is Deer. My birth star (Purvabhadra) animal is Lion. She smiled back saying that my claw was becoming very sharp too. Smiling repartee gets smiling response. I would certainly plead guilty if someone said that I was trying to use less harsh words about her responses because of my love for her. Well, that's how she trained me. Actually I always said she was a good husband-trainer, and a good dog-trainer.

The word dog rings a bell. I am not a great lover of canine beings. The humans appeal to me; non-humans don't enamour me. Why beat around the bush? A dog held my calf between its teeth, when I was about six years old. That must have been responsible for my nonpositive feeling towards canines. Well, let me be honest: most of my kith and kin share this nonpositive feeling for canine beings. On the other hand Her Majesty the Queen of Massachusetts did have positive feelings for canine beings. In general feelings of courage and non-timidity, she was much better placed than me. I would like to say with a good amount of certainty that this kind of positive feelings towards canine beings and others is also part of her cognizance and rationality. There is a reason for saying this. My son and I realized that we should rationalize our fear to get off it. He has a wonderful dog at home called Leo. To be honest, my wife felt close to him but I did not. One may wonder why I called my wife queen. Her name is Rajyalakshmi which can be translated as "the goddess of the realm", which can be rendered as the queen. I also used to say that she was the queen of my heart. Our two year stay in England did make a qualitative change in my vocatives. I used to call her 'darling' and 'beauty' more often than Raja, her shortened name. She used to call me darling too, besides 'ēmandi' (what sir). Several of my relatives and friends emulated me and called their wives darling. One might wonder whether the vocatives reflect inner reality. Here we can go back to Plato who said that acting becomes second nature of man and so vocatives may ultimately determine the inner reality too.

This kind of platonic love must have really created agape between us, a love without any gap, a love without any motive, a love without any question. This togetherness made us read many books together. We read Mahabharata, Bhagavat Puran, Ramayana and some Upanishads together. Some of her comments did surprise me with their depth. Regarding the Mahabharata she said: "When someone is born someone else is born to kill him and a cause is there for it." One of her comments moved me almost to tears of happiness. We were reading Valmiki Ramayana together. There an incident refers to a dialogue between Kaikeyi and Rama. The Queen Kaikeyi wanted Rama to leave for the forest for fourteen years. While discussing something else she asked him to get ready to go. Rama replied, "Ramo dvibhasbhar nate" which means 'Rama doesn't say two (contradictory) things'. My wife said: "You are also like that, right? You don't go back on your word." This was really a moving certificate which very few queens might be kind enough to issue to their consorts.

Our reading of Ramayana (in Telugu), rendered into Telugu by Padma Sri Pullela Sriramachandrudu, led to an abridged summary of Valmiki which was published with us as co-authors. Way back in 1985 I had come out with a lyrical summary of the Bhagavad Gita (Telugu). I have just come out with Sri Krishnayanam (in Telugu) based on the ninth, tenth and eleventh cantos of the Bhagavatpuran.

The queen's smile and matching responses really were a blessing for me. She would never protest too much. I would certainly feel happy to refer to the incident which made me interpret the expression UPS to suit me. I came back from the university and wanted a cup of coffee. I don't remember whether I got my coffee or not but she gave me a shopping bag and asked me to bring some vegetables. I took the bag and walked to the shop which was half a kilometre away, bought the vegetables and started walking back. On my way back it occurred to me that she would have to pay a servant boy if she had asked him to bring vegetables, and now that I am her husband she would not pay me. Then it occurred to me that a helping and loving husband is UPS, which meant Unpaid Primary Servant of the house. If he is a bad husband he is Uninterrupted Pain Supplier. Forgive me, if he is like me a good husband he is Uninterrupted Pleasure Supplier. I made this UPS concept of Unpaid Primary Servant of the house very popular; she never protested; she just smiled it off. And a smile can be interpreted anyway but my presence was for her a must. She was sure of one thing: I could anticipate her needs and fulfil them whereas her children could not guess what she wanted. Generally speaking she would not ask for anything. She would 'oblige us by accepting what we offer'. This was the comment of one of my grand-daughters, who knew the nature of their clan. This grand-daughter one day asked her why she kept quiet even when I said something she didn't like. The queen's reply was unbeatable, she said: "That is **maryada**". This word 'maryada' seems to reflect good manners, courteous behaviour, affability, good breeding and observance of devoir.

Her graceful behaviour personified this ***maryada***.